PRAISE FOR *GOOD LISTEN*

"In *Good Listen*, Joe Pardavila shares his wisdom and experiences on how talking less and listening more can have a profound positive impact on our personal and professional life. It's a must-read for anyone who wants to learn the secrets of effective listening."

—MICHAEL CLINTON
Author of ROAR: into the second half of your life

"In today's world, we all know we are more connected than we've ever been in history, which is why it's such a surprise when we realize how disconnected we feel. The connections are wide, but they're not deep. We can send a quick hello to our family group text, or have a Zoom happy hour with our college friends, but those good conversations—those deep, soul-baring, vulnerable and healing talks—are harder to come by as we search for the perfect GIF. Joe Pardavila has spent his career having conversations with fascinating people, and his knack for connection takes those talks into unexpected and engaging places. Let him tell you what he's learned so that you can use it in your life and regain the human connection you've been missing. As you would expect from Joe, *Good Listen* is a very good hang."

—DAVE HOLMES
Editor-at-Large, Esquire

"Communicating effectively is a superpower. If you want to sharpen your skills, understand others better, and get your own message heard, *Good Listen* provides invaluable advice."

—DORIE CLARK
Wall Street Journal *bestselling author of* The Long Game; *executive education faculty, Duke University Fuqua School of Business*

"In a time when social media 'conversations' amount to 280 characters or memes, it's reassuring to see that Joe is reminding all of us that there's no innovation that can take the place of a meaningful, person-to-person conversation. He reminds us that curiosity, asking thoughtful questions, and being a great listener opens all of us to learning more and making meaningful connections."

—SANDY GIRARD
Executive Vice President, Programming, Crooked Media

"*Good Listen* takes us on a jaunty adventure down the central path by which humans connect with each other—conversation—with an expert talker as our guide. Pardavila's book is a 'good read' for anyone who wants to both smile and learn along the way."

—ALISON WOOD BROOKS
Professor, Harvard Business School

"I've worked in the audio space from the days when it was only radio to today, when audio is everywhere and hotter than ever in these new smart times. This book shows why audio still matters, and despite the changes that have happened within radio, there is still an enthusiasm for the sound of sound. Joe shares his journey from the kid in college to today where he is recognized for what he was involved in creating and what his contributions have become. I'm honored to have been able to work with him and see firsthand the magic that he created."

—MIKE McVAY
President, McVay Media Consulting

GOOD
LISTEN

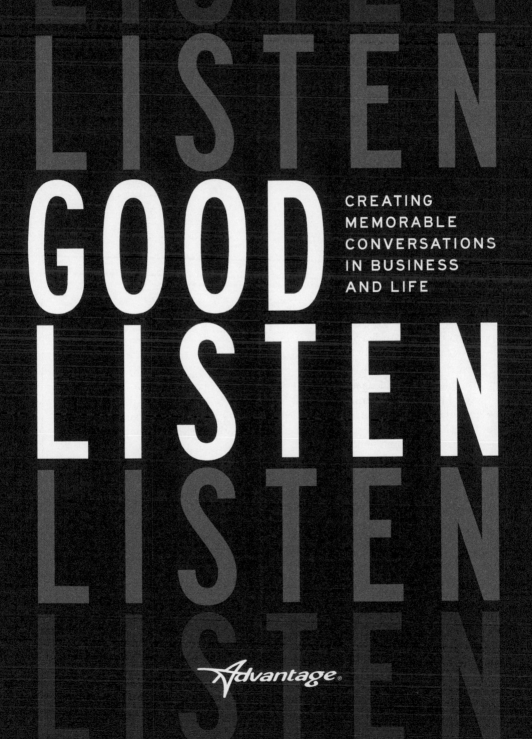

JOE PARDAVILA

GOOD LISTEN

CREATING
MEMORABLE
CONVERSATIONS
IN BUSINESS
AND LIFE

Advantage®

Published by Advantage, Charleston, South Carolina.
Member of Advantage Media Group.

ADVANTAGE is a registered trademark, and the Advantage colophon is a trademark of Advantage Media Group, Inc.

Printed in the United States of America.

10 9 8 7 6 5 4 3 2 1

ISBN: 978-1-64225-384-9
LCCN: 2022902425

Cover design by Analisa Smith.
Back cover photo by Chris Lonsberry.

This publication is designed to provide accurate and authoritative information in regard to the subject matter covered. It is sold with the understanding that the publisher is not engaged in rendering legal, accounting, or other professional services. If legal advice or other expert assistance is required, the services of a competent professional person should be sought.

Advantage Media Group is proud to be a part of the Tree Neutral® program. Tree Neutral offsets the number of trees consumed in the production and printing of this book by taking proactive steps such as planting trees in direct proportion to the number of trees used to print books. To learn more about Tree Neutral, please visit **www.treeneutral.com**.

Advantage Media Group is a publisher of business, self-improvement, and professional development books and online learning. We help entrepreneurs, business leaders, and professionals share their Stories, Passion, and Knowledge to help others Learn & Grow. Do you have a manuscript or book idea that you would like us to consider for publishing? Please visit **advantagefamily.com**.

To Theresa and Mom.

CONTENTS

INTRODUCTION 1
THE POWER OF CONVERSATION

CHAPTER 1 9
INTERNET KILLED THE RADIO STAR

CHAPTER 2 25
CREATING MAGIC MOMENTS

CHAPTER 3 33
THE SECRET TO CONVERSATIONAL SUCCESS

CHAPTER 4 47
IF YOU'RE DOING MORE TALKING THAN LISTENING, YOU'RE DOING IT WRONG

CHAPTER 5 59
SHARING IS CARING

CHAPTER 6 69
"YES, AND ..."

CHAPTER 7 79
TAKE YOURSELF TO AN ELEVEN

CHAPTER 8 89

PREPARATION, CONCENTRATION, MODERATION

CHAPTER 9 105

AVOIDING DIALOGUE DISASTERS

CHAPTER 10 119

THE YIN AND YANG OF PODCASTS

AFTERWORD 137

SIMPLE AWARENESS

ACKNOWLEDGMENTS 141

DONE-FOR-YOU PODCASTING SERVICES 143

LISTEN

LISTEN

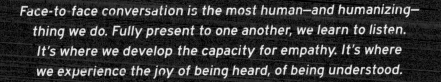

Face-to-face conversation is the most human—and humanizing—
thing we do. Fully present to one another, we learn to listen.
It's where we develop the capacity for empathy. It's where
we experience the joy of being heard, of being understood.

—PSYCHOLOGIST SHERRY TURKLE

LISTEN

LISTEN

THE POWER OF CONVERSATION

FOR MY ENTIRE PROFESSIONAL CAREER, my goal has always been to give people a "good listen."

That's because it was, and still is, a big part of my job description, starting with my radio career. Remember radio? The thing you plug your iPhone into? Maybe on your way to work, you used to listen to your local morning team of DJs who brought you weather, traffic, and news sandwiched in between comedy bits, celebrity interviews, and a few crazy sound effects just to break things up. Well, that's where you would have found me if you lived in the New York City area and tuned in to 95.5 WPLJ-FM (or 'PLJ, as we called it at the time).

That was where I really learned my craft—how to effectively communicate and connect with people. For over twenty years, I was part of WPLJ's successful morning team, where we interviewed all sorts of celebs and newsmakers. People like Ed Sheeran, Lady Gaga, Justin Bieber, Kevin Bacon, Mike Tyson, and Kim Kardashian regularly showed up in our studio to, yeah, promote a project and to talk with us for a few minutes. We used those few minutes to try and get something unexpected and surprising from our special guest star of

Me and just a few of the celebrities I had the privilege of meeting through my work at 95.5 'PLJ

the day. A lot of the time, we succeeded, and I'll be sharing a few of those experiences throughout these pages.

But I want to be clear—this book isn't about talking to stars. It's about talking to *anyone*, including the guy at the counter of your neighborhood 7-Eleven if you're so inclined. Hey, you might find out a few fascinating facts about Slurpees. What is that stuff spinning around in those glass cases? What's it made of? That should take up five minutes or so.

There is a certain power to conversation if you do it right, even with that 7-Eleven clerk. As a matter of fact, the most important and memorable conversations I ever had on the air were with hundreds of ordinary New Yorkers on one traumatic day—September 11, 2001.

That morning, a beautiful late summer day, we were doing our usual show, completely unaware that the city was about to be shaken to its core. Inside our studio our TV monitors were set to WABC-TV, the local ABC affiliate, because their weatherman was also our weatherman, Bill Evans, who's been on the air in NYC for decades—he would pop in periodically during the broadcast to give our listeners the latest forecast. But then one of us glanced at the screen and noticed something very, very shocking—smoke was billowing out of one of the Twin Towers. WABC quickly reported what had happened—a plane had hit the iconic building, and as a result it was on fire. Accident? Maybe. Nobody was sure what was going on. But when the second plane hit the other tower, we all suddenly knew.

Our city was under attack.

Suddenly the whole vibe of our show changed. It obviously had to, as we were dealing with a terrorist strike the likes of which had never been seen before. The calls started pouring in. People didn't know whether their family members had survived. Others were caught in the heavy smoke and debris falling from the sky, not really understanding what was happening. Instantly we were taking calls left and right from confused and traumatized folks who were looking for answers. Here's a sample exchange during our show from that shocking day as events were just unfolding:

> **CALLER #1:** The building is exploding right now. You got people running up the street. I don't know what's going on!

> **CALLER #2:** It looked to me like there was a jet airliner that just turned right into it again.

> **SCOTT SHANNON:** Well, if, if you just flipped the radio on—it's a little after nine o'clock—this is WPLJ New York. Scott & Todd in the Morning. There is a horrible disaster. That was a second hit. Confirmed. Now another plane. That building is under attack.

> **CALLER #3:** It's the south tower. This is terrorism.

Later on, people were desperately trying to find their loved ones. We tried to help.

> **CALLER #4:** I wanted to make a plea. My brother worked for Cantor Fitzgerald. He was on the 104th floor, and all the calls that we're making, we're not getting very much turnout for Cantor people. If anybody saw him anywhere, or if anybody from Cantor got out, if they could call us and just tell us something, just anything.

You can find more excerpts from that horrible unforgettable morning on YouTube.

We were one of the few places people could call for help, as the internet was not nearly as ubiquitous as it is now. Not only that, but also most cell phones weren't working because of equipment damage and network overload. So it was up to us to pass on every piece of information we learned. And when we couldn't answer a question, we tried to reach someone who could.

In a sense, we were the audience's surrogates because we were watching everything unfold live, just as they were, and we were just as upset as they were. It was almost like therapy for our callers to be able to talk to us and try to make some kind of sense out of what was happening, even though that ask was virtually impossible. How do you logically explain something so insane?

We tried for hours and hours. Our morning shift stretched into the afternoon and then continued into the night because the city had closed down, and none of the other DJs could make it to the studio to take over for us. We ended up being on the air from 6:00 a.m. to 8:00 p.m., fourteen hours in all, but we had enough adrenaline flowing that I'm sure we could have kept going into the next morning. As it was I had to crash at a friend's place that night because I couldn't get back home.

Of all the years I worked on the show, nothing ever bonded all of us together like that day did. We were totally focused on our mission, which was to help as many people as we could through the tragedy, and in the process we found ourselves suddenly connecting with our audience in ways we never imagined. We were used to entertaining people, but that day it was all about supporting a community that needed consoling and, just as importantly, some hope to hang on to. Years later I still run into people on the street who bring up 9/11 and remember how they listened to us all day long.

Because it was such an unforgettable experience, it's strange to think that what happened on the air that day can never happen again. The media landscape has changed radically, and if, God forbid, another attack happened on our country's soil, most people would be communicating online through social media, not trying to get through to a radio station to talk to their local DJ. For one thing there might not even be a local DJ around anymore—at least one who's on the air live.

The fact is I didn't leave radio; radio left me. WPLJ was sold to a Christian broadcasting company in 2019, so you might say I was fired by Jesus. Now it's basically a satellite station simulcasting canned broadcasts. The result? I'm no longer able to communicate with thousands and thousands of people simultaneously. Yeah, that feels like a loss. But there was a big gain in the aftermath as well. Now I have the privilege to connect with people at a deeper level than ever before. As the director and host of podcasts for ForbesBooks and Advantage Media Group, I guide people from all walks of life in how to share their expertise, as well as their life struggles and triumphs, through compelling conversation. So I still get to reach thousands of people, only now they're listening when it's convenient for them, not when I happen to be on radio broadcasting.

In a way this transition has been reassuring. I previously thought the art of conversation might have been going the way of the dodo and the DeLorean. After all most people now communicate through texts, chats, and emails, and emotions, of course, have been boiled down to emojis. But podcasts at the moment are ruling the day, and better yet they have brought back the concept of creating a "good listen"—memorable conversation that can inform and entertain, just like my old buddies and I used to do on the radio but stripped down and simpler. You may call it "ordinary talk," the kind all of us do, whether we're interacting with friends and family, work associates, or whomever.

But here's the thing. That talk doesn't have to be ordinary. It can be exciting, revealing, emotional, and even surprising—if you know how to make that talk as memorable and interesting as possible. That's the idea that gave birth to this book. It occurred to me that a lot of other people out there may need the same kind of advice I give to newsmakers, CEOs, and other accomplished professionals on how to make their talk count—because this advice applies not only to podcasts but also to life conversations that can be crucial. I'm talking job interviews. Relationships. Family interactions. Sales. Dates. Work meetings. And of course chatting with that 7-Eleven clerk. How else are you going to find out what the Powerball jackpot is for that week?

So if you're one of those people who want to create a "good listen" in your professional or private life, keep turning the pages because they're full of easy tips and tricks that will not only help you do well on your side of the conversation but will also inspire the other person to up their game.

Contrary to the cliché, talk isn't cheap. It's a very valuable commodity. And you're about to learn how to leverage that commodity and collect a lifetime of dividends.

CHAPTER 1

INTERNET KILLED THE RADIO STAR
HOW COMMUNICATION AIN'T WHAT IT USED TO BE

I'M FAR FROM THE OLDEST GUY in the world, which is a good thing because it's not a title you hold on to for very long. But still, as a Gen Xer, I've seen a seismic change in my lifetime. The internet, in particular, turned the world upside down, especially when it comes to how we communicate. In this first chapter, I'd like to talk about that big change, how it affected how we all connect with each other, and how I watched it all happen during my career in radio. This is all important because it not only informs the rest of the book, but you'll also understand how I learned everything I know about how to create a "good listen."

When Society Stopped Talking the Talk (Or at Least Cut Down on It)

It all used to be a lot simpler.

Before the internet and cell phones began to rule our lives, if you wanted to call someone, you had one choice: a landline. At home you would use the one in your house, and if you were out and about, you had to find a pay phone booth, the kind Superman used to change clothes in (at superspeed so he wouldn't get arrested for exposing himself, I would guess). Now it's difficult to find a working pay phone anywhere, and as for home landlines, the stats are startling. In 2004 over 90 percent of households in the United States had one, but by 2020 that figure had plummeted to only 40 percent.[1]

You could say that *of course* that's the case. After all we use smartphones to make calls now instead of landlines, and they're small enough to carry around in our pockets. So big deal, right? What's the difference? Well, here's the difference. We're talking *less* on those smartphones. One study showed that 80 percent of cell phone users made calls that were shorter than five minutes, and most were under ninety seconds. A total of 6 percent of them never made a single call.[2] And you know why that is, right? Because most of us primarily text now. It saves time and money, and if you just have a quick message to deliver, it's perfect.

But what's also true is that a lot is lost when we don't actually communicate primarily through conversation. Texts (and emails and online chats too) can seem cold and impersonal or even unintentionally hostile when a comment or joke is misunderstood and comes across as insulting. How much is lost? Well, UCLA professor Albert Mehrabian found that 58 percent of communication is through body language; 35 percent through vocal tone, pitch, and emphasis; and only 7 percent through the content of the message![3]

---

1   Ethen Kim Lieser, "Study: Only 40 Percent of U.S. Households Have a Landline," *National Interest*, March 20, 2020, https://nationalinterest.org/blog/buzz/study-only-40-percent-us-households-have-landline-135212.

2   Rebecca Nicholson, "The Lost Art of Having a Chat," *Guardian*, February 9, 2020, https://www.theguardian.com/global/2020/feb/09/the-lost-art-of-having-a-chat.

3   Kim Schneiderman, "The Trouble with Texting," *Psychology Today*, January 21, 2013, https://www.psychologytoday.com/us/blog/the-novel-perspective/201301/the-trouble-texting.

So if you buy those numbers, that means you're only communicating less than 10 percent of what you want to say by tapping out texts on your smartphone's keypad. That's kind of frightening. I mean, only 7 percent of the intent gets through in a text? How is that acceptable? Imagine a football coach trying to motivate his players by saying, "C'mon, guys, we've got to give this game 7 percent!" That could explain the Jets's recent seasons, but still …

A lot is lost when we don't actually communicate primarily through conversation.

Anyway, as I said, I grew up watching this evolution firsthand because it affected the course of my career as well as a lot of other people's. Talking is how I've always made my living, and it's how I made my way to becoming part of a top radio morning team in the number one market in the United States—New York City. It didn't happen because I had connections or any kind of formal training. Nor did it happen because I had a lot of resources. My brother and I were the children of immigrants. My mom was a Cuban refugee who was able to come to the United States in the late 1960s with nothing but the clothes on her back, while my dad was a ship mechanic from Spain who decided to settle down in the States, where he met my mom. They worked hard to make ends meet, twice as hard as most parents had to, so they could give us whatever we needed or wanted.

In other words, besides my parents' love and support, I had absolutely nothing going for me. So how was I able to become a radio professional? Well, my first lucky break was this: God made me and my brother Arturo lousy at sports. We loved them (as a matter of fact, today Arturo is a VP with Major League Baseball Advanced Media), but to be blunt we sucked at them. As a result I got heavily into the pop culture of the time, constantly watching TV shows and movies. When I was growing up, my friends and even my brother loved athletes like Don Mattingly and Joe Montana. Me? My hero was David Letterman because that dude was always breaking the rules and making it work for him. And that was who I wanted to be. My father ended up being a machinist and worked in the GE building (now 30 Rock) for a time, where Letterman did his show. And he actually got me his autograph, which was a hard get.

But other than that, a kid like me growing up in New Jersey didn't have many outlets for those kinds of dreams. The high school I went to was so small it didn't have a TV or radio station where I could at least try out my ambitions. All I managed to achieve was becoming the PA announcer at the basketball games during my last two years there. Well, at least I was broadcasting my voice, even if it was only to the fifty or sixty people in the stands.

And that's what I cared about. I can't say my classes kept my interest. My grades weren't great (Bs and Cs) because I would rather play video games and watch TV than study, and luckily I was just smart enough to get away with that. So I wasn't about to get a scholarship to an Ivy League school or anything close after I graduated. My options again were very, *very* limited, and I ended up going to a state college in Jersey, William Patterson College (now a university), which I picked because they had a communications program. My first day on the campus, I was excited to see they had a TV station. But the people running that station were not excited to see me because only juniors and seniors got to sit in front of the cameras. So I had to settle for radio. I managed to get a shift at the college station because, frankly, not many others wanted to do it. Well, as you'll find out, when I see an opening, I tend to run through it. So radio it was, even though TV talk shows were still my true love.

*At my first real radio gig as part of college station 88.7
WPSC-FM, alongside station manager and advisor John Kiernan
and fellow student Rich Kaminski, who would go on to have a
long-running career on 106.7 Lite FM in New York.*

But there was a nice surprise in store for me—I ended up loving
my radio experience. The problem was I wanted to do it for real, not
on a college campus. So I started applying for internships during my
sophomore year and got accepted for a couple of them in New York
City. I had to choose which one to take, and that was a little scary.
When you grow up in Jersey and you're from a working-class family,
NYC seems like an overwhelming and intimidating place. I never
went there unless my parents took me to see the Christmas lights or
something. With that in mind, I chose the internship at WPLJ. Why?
Because their studios were right above Penn Station. I could take
the train straight there from home and take it right back when I was
finished. Yes, I based my decision on convenience. Not many careers
are based on "Well, this'll be easy," but mine was.

I put everything into that internship since it was a pathway to ... well, *something*, but I had no idea what. However, when my internship was about up, there happened to be a vacancy in WPLJ's promotion department. The job was to drive to events in the station van and hand out T-shirts and other station swag. (This was back when radio stations could afford swag, not to mention a promotion department.) And they needed to fill the position *immediately*. Again, I saw an opening, and I ran through it.

But there was a slight hiccup. They told me, "Well, if you took the job, you'd have to quit school. This is a full-time gig." So I had to stop and think a moment. Okay, that's a lie. I didn't have to think at all. I instantly put college in my rearview mirror and said, "I don't care. Sign me up."

I quickly thought about ways to make my new job more fun, both for me and the general public. Like Letterman, I wanted to break some rules. So when I went to events for giveaways, I started using gimmicks I had seen at carnivals and the like. For example, I would ask a crowd of hundreds of people if anyone wanted me to guess how old they were. Suddenly everyone was screaming for me to estimate their age. I began to get good at crowd work, culminating in that magic moment when one of the station DJs saw what I was doing and told me I was doing a good job and that I had a bright future ahead of me. A good sign. And an even better one than I thought at the time ... because a few months later, management decided to shake up the morning show staff, and they asked me to be a part of the new crew.

This was something I never dreamed would happen to me. I was suddenly part of a top five NYC morning radio show. But my role was not all that exciting. Basically I screened the host's phone calls to find out stuff in advance so they would know what to talk about on air with the caller. In other words I was a glorified phone operator, banished to what was called "the phone pit," a small room adjacent to the big studio, where all the hosts and guests would sit. There was still a closed door standing between me and what I considered big-time showbiz.

But this was where my education paid off. Please note I'm not talking about anything that happened in a school I attended; I'm talking about my hours and hours of watching TV as a kid. The hosts realized that I was an insane trivia freak who could answer almost any obscure pop culture question that came up when they were on the air. (This was a year or so before Larry Page and Sergey Brin came up with the Google thing.) When that happened, they would go to me in the phone pit to ask for the answer. And because I delivered, I was soon moved out of the pit and into the studio, a promotion that had a price.

That price was accepting my new name. As you can tell from the book cover, my name is Joe, but Joe was also the name of the station's traffic guy, a broadcaster named Joe Nolan. Everyone thought it would be confusing having two Joes on the air at once because it was radio, and a listener wouldn't be able to tell one Joe from the other. So Scott and Todd, the hosts, figured I needed a wacky nickname. Well, one of the morning shows in Philadelphia, just down I-95 from us, had a character named Monkey Boy. So they came to me and asked, "What do you think about us calling you Monkey Boy?" Another opening I ran through. My instant response was "Hey, you can call me anything you want!"

To be honest I figured I'd be there just another couple of years at most, and then I could shed the nickname. Little did I know, twenty years later, I'd still be there. But a good thing happened after a couple of years to alleviate this Monkey Boy's pain. Everyone was too lazy to keep saying my whole nickname, so they started shortening it up to just plain Monk. And from there I kept getting promoted, first to associate producer and then executive producer. I ended up in charge of the entire show, booking the guests, prepping the show, and whatever else needed to be done. In my last few years, I was a bona fide cohost.

In any event that time period was when I got my real education.

The Scott and Todd School

I've been using the term "hosts" pretty generically up until now, but the truth is the two I ended up working with were the best of the best in the business. The morning show at that time was called "Scott and Todd" because of the heavyweight combo who hosted the show.

"Scott" was Scott Shannon, a guy who made millions in his prime—and that was from local radio alone. He's in the Rock and Roll Hall of Fame, the National Radio Hall of Fame, and the National Association of Broadcasters Hall of Fame and is still doing radio as I write these words. This guy was born for radio, and he knew it. Here's how he reacted to his first on-air gig:

> I'll never forget when I first started. I was in the US Army in Columbus, Georgia. And I moonlighted at a radio station, and we broadcasted from a transmitter because the owner was very cheap. And when I would play a song, I don't know why I did this, but I would walk outside on the gravel road outside the station, which was just a little cinder block hut with a transmitter and a little microphone, and look up at the big tower with the blinking lights. And I'd think to myself, "Holy cow, people all over Georgia and Alabama are listening to me. And my voice is coming out of that damn tower." I'd stare at that tower, not just once but all the time. "How the hell is that working? I don't get it. That's amazing," I'd think to myself.

"Todd" was Todd Pettengill, and he was no slouch either. When he became cohost of the WPLJ morning show, he was the youngest morning show host in New York radio at the age of twenty-five. He made *Billboard* magazine Major Market Air personality of the year six times and Radio & Records Major Market Air personality of the year four times. I mean, the only award I ever won was for our seventh-grade lip sync contest, when I borrowed my cousin's guitar and did "Born in the U.S.A." (And I think I only won because I was three feet tall, and the guitar was about five feet long—it was an outstanding visual.)

It was my privilege to work with these pros each and every day, and unlike high school I actually learned things. I saw what worked and what didn't work. When something they did flopped, I kept my mouth shut but my mind open and made a note of it. When you're doing a show like that day in and day out, you can't help but learn, and a lot of the knowledge I soaked up is in this book. These guys had to function at a high level. They had to communicate effectively, had to keep their audience listening, or they would have ended up in Des Moines radio doing the farm report at 5:00 a.m. And I'm not sure either of them knew much about corn, wheat, or pork bellies.

Even though Scott and Todd got the bulk of the airtime, I was on the air every day interacting with them. I had to build up my own skills and keep things moving (especially when I took on a producer role). I learned a lot just by, as the famous *Hamilton* song puts it, "being in the room." When you're on the air for four hours, three hundred days a year, you can't help but elevate your game.

It was my privilege to work with these pros each and every day, and unlike high school I actually learned things.

But then the radio landscape began to change, and not for the better.

Behind the scenes at 95.5 'PLJ (with Todd Pettengill).

When News Was No Longer News

As my radio career progressed, so did the power of the internet. And that impacted our show big time. In the early days, we would read three or four local NY papers and some national ones like *USA Today*, then we would talk about the stuff in the papers that was interesting, hilarious, or just plain weird. Our listeners wouldn't have time to consume all that before their morning commutes, so most of what we talked about was news to them. At the time it was called "infotainment," and it drove our show.

But then we experienced the first warning sign that web surfing was about to wash our profession away.

People were now going online and finding out all the news and celebrity gossip that was an integral part of our show on their own. By the time we started talking about it, it was already stale. We were aware there was a growing problem, but we didn't know what to do about it. There was kind of an unspoken rule in our studio—no talk about personal stuff unless somebody got married or had a baby, some big, positive event that needed to be recognized. Well, we had to throw that rule out the door because talking about what was going on in our lives was the only way we had left to surprise and intrigue our audience.

And in a way that transition paved the way for my future transition to podcasting. I had to learn how to make those kinds of personal conversations interesting and entertaining. It wasn't easy, but I was always on the lookout to make even the most basic celebrity interview take an unexpected turn.

Quick example: We had Adam Levine from Maroon 5 on. And if you remember his band had been huge when they first popped up, putting out hit after hit, but then their success faded. White guys with guitars were suddenly out of fashion. That's the music business—most bands come and go. But when he talked with us, Maroon 5 and Adam were both in the midst of a huge comeback. He had joined the judging panel on *The Voice*, an instant reality TV smash, and put out a duet with Christina Aguilera, "Moves Like Jagger," which went to number one. Adam was back with a vengeance.

Now it's no secret that Adam Levine can come off as the cockiest dude on the planet. I wanted to get past that facade, so I asked him, "Can you imagine yourself being where you are now if you didn't have this opportunity to be on *The Voice*? Do you think you would have still been able to get back in the spotlight?"

And then surprisingly he opened up about that difficult time. He said to me, "No, I probably couldn't have because I didn't know what I didn't know. I was the lead singer of Maroon 5—no one could tell me anything. And to be honest I was humbled by what happened. And it made me realize I couldn't do it all by myself. Our band did need help. We needed other songwriters. We needed new producers." And he was right because when he opened himself up to other creative voices, Maroon 5 went on an unprecedented run, where they had top ten hits for a decade or so. To date, the band has sold more than 135 million records, making them one of the world's best-selling music artists.

Getting Adam Levine to admit he had been humbled was something of a coup. But it wouldn't have happened if my question didn't come naturally out of the conversation we were having. I listened closely to what he was saying (I'm big on listening, as you'll find out), tapped into his vibe, and let him lead me to that moment.

This was a process that came in mighty handy for my next evolution.

From Broadcasting to Podcasting

In 1522 Magellan's expedition returned to Spain after a journey of forty-four thousand miles. It took three years and cost the lives of almost all the crew members, Magellan included.[4]

---

4   Yuval Noah Harari, *Sapiens: A Brief History of Humankind* (Harper, 2015).

That lines up with what happened to radio over the past decade or so.

As the radio audience numbers began to fall off a cliff, Scott left WPLJ in 2014. Todd stayed on until the station's sale and sign-off in 2019, as did I. You couldn't help but see the writing on the wall, so a couple of years before the station was sold, I began to look for a new career. My current one was becoming obsolete—radio was more into firing than hiring by then.

At the time, however, podcasting was already in full swing. The radio station management had us do a little bit of it here and there, but nothing much came of it. I knew I needed to try it on my own. I had gotten pretty good at interviews, and I knew the format would suit my talents. The question was, what kind of podcast would I do? What would be interesting to other people and grab their attention?

Well, like countless others before me, I went on the premise that sex sells.

For my podcast I wanted to find subject matter we could never do on the radio, where content was mostly PG and family friendly, aside from a little innuendo here and there. My thought was to do something I never could have done on WPLJ. So I became friends with a professor at NYU, Dr. Zhana Vrangalova, a scientist who taught classes in relationships and sex. And I told her I would love to do a show where little old me, just this normal guy, takes deep dives into sexuality with a genuine expert. She went along with the idea, and soon our *Science of Sex* podcast was happening. Sure enough the concept sparked a lot of publicity and interest. We ended up interviewing other PhDs and professors about all sorts of interesting things, as you can tell from a sampling of our non-PG podcast titles, such as "How to Get a PhD in Threesomes," "Orgasms for Dummies," "How Kinky Is Too Kinky?" "Do Sluttier People Make Worse Romantic Partners?" and "Sex-Question Palooza."

Recording the Science of Sex *podcast with Dr. Zhana Vrangalova*

To say I learned a lot is an understatement. But I soon realized my role was not only to react to what Dr. Zhana and our guests were saying (and they were usually saying plenty) but also to "translate" their academic speak to the listeners. Every expert flirts (is that the wrong word to use about a sex expert?) with jargon, and most people, including me, don't understand it. "Hold on a second," I'd say. "No one understands what any of these acronyms mean." So I would ask her to explain in more everyday language what she was talking about, enabling us to connect more effectively with our audience.

The podcast was a great experience. It was the first time in my career that the strings were cut. Usually we only had six minutes total for a conversation on the radio. Now I had up to an hour to discuss cosplay and other weighty topics. The extra time just gave the conversations room to breathe. The other thing was that radio (especially morning radio back then) required you to be a little more aggressive.

You kind of had to be in people's faces to wake them up and keep them listening with all the bells and whistles you had at your disposal (and sometimes they were literally bells and whistles). Podcasting was refreshing because the tone was different—a little more NPR and much less morning zoo. It was still about performance, as we'll discuss later, but at a more real-life level.

Just doing sixty or so episodes of that podcast taught me a lot. I discovered I could leverage my existing communication skills to work in that medium. I learned what worked and what didn't in this new medium. And ultimately it was the perfect way to train for my current position at ForbesBooks as podcast director. Many of our authors appear on our podcasts, and I host and walk them through it. What I like to tell them is, "The book is your Bible, and your podcast is your Sunday sermon." It's an opportunity to showcase their expertise and possibly motivate listeners to maybe buy their books.

That's where I am now. It's an exciting position to be in. I get to interact with a lot of smart and accomplished people and help them connect with a larger audience. And again it all comes out of conducting conversations that communicate important ideas and interesting facts and enjoying the journey.

So that's enough about me. And while I'll share some relevant anecdotes from my career in the pages to come, it'll be for the purpose of accentuating points and providing context. This book is all about how to have the best conversations possible, whether you're doing a podcast, at work, or at home with friends and family. Specifically I'm going to share the most important tips and tricks I've learned over the years that have made an incredible difference to me and will, I believe, to you as well.

Let's face it. Talk is routinely dismissed in our culture. Action is much more valued, with the implication being that talking doesn't accomplish anything. Well, I have to disagree. Talk educates, informs, and gives you new perspectives to take in and incisive insights that can reverberate throughout your life. And if you do it right, you can make a living at it just like I do. If that's your goal, I'm about to put you ahead of the game because you're about to find out what it took me twenty-five years or so to learn.

> Talk educates, informs, and gives you new perspectives to take in and incisive insights that can reverberate throughout your life. And if you do it right, you can make a living at it just like I do.

Just turn the page, and class will be in session. But one small favor—please pay more attention in this class than I did in high school.

CHAPTER 2

CREATING MAGIC MOMENTS
FINDING WAYS TO MAKE YOUR CONVERSATIONS STAND OUT

"THIS MAGIC MOMENT ... so different and so new ..."

You may recognize those opening lyrics from an old rock classic by the Drifters because the song, "This Magic Moment," is used frequently on commercials. For example, as I write these words, it's used in a TV campaign promoting almond-crusted chicken for a nationwide Chinese food chain. The allure for advertisers is obvious—everyone loves to experience a "magic moment," so why not promise one? (I'll leave it up to you if almond-crusted chicken qualifies as magical.)

But why do people love to experience magic moments? Well, because they're unexpected, out of the ordinary, and memorable and powerful. We seek them out in our lives to elevate our experiences, and when we see the potential for them, we chase after them. I'm here to give you a leg up on that pursuit, which is why, throughout the rest of this book, you'll learn the best techniques to make them happen.

Magic moments can pay big dividends. In a personal interchange, a magic moment can create a special and unique bond between you and the other person. In a podcast, if a magic moment is big enough, it will generate buzz and spike interest in what you're doing. And if it happens in a video interview, the right magic moment can go viral and raise your profile as well as your platform. That's why I believe magic moments are the ultimate when it comes to providing a "good listen." And the best thing about them is there is so little downside to going for them and so much upside if you end up creating one.

With that in mind, let's dig into magic moments—what they're all about and how we can create the conditions for making them happen.

William Goldman, Paul Newman, and Bad Coffee

You may not know the name William Goldman, but he was one of Hollywood's most famous screenwriters, winning two Oscars, one for *Butch Cassidy and the Sundance Kid* and one for *All the President's Men*. He also wrote a whole bunch of other classics, such as *The Princess Bride*, *Marathon Man*, and *Misery*. All these movies are filled with magic moments, but it took some time until Goldman truly understood their power. To be exact, it took until his second produced screenplay, which was for the Paul Newman detective flick, *Harper*.

And it almost didn't happen.

While *Harper* was being filmed, Goldman got a desperate last-minute call from the producer, who had just realized he needed a scene to run under the opening credits. (This was back when there *were* opening credits in movies.) So Goldman quickly typed up (this was also back when there were typewriters) a scene of Newman getting up in the morning and getting ready for the day. It didn't seem like anything special to him, but it would serve its purpose of giving the audience something to look at while the credits went by.

Then the movie was released. Great reviews, great box office. Yet Goldman was confused. Everyone kept telling him over and over how much they loved the part with the coffee. Goldman would graciously thank them, but in his head he kept thinking, "What part with the coffee?"

He had already seen the movie in a private screening, but he decided he needed to see it with a crowd so he could find out what was generating this kind of response. So he went to a theater where *Harper* was playing and watched the opening scene he had banged out in a few minutes just to get it done. In the scene Paul Newman goes into the kitchen and discovers he's out of coffee. He's not happy about that. He spots some old grounds, still in a filter, sitting on top of the garbage. He shrugs, fishes the grounds out, makes coffee with them, takes a sip … and then makes the most disgusted face in the history of cinema. The audience erupted in laughter. Goldman was still perplexed—okay, Newman was great in the scene, but *this* was what people thought was such a big deal?

Then he realized that was in fact a magic moment that made everyone instantly love Paul Newman's character. From then on they were willing to go along with whatever Newman did in the movie; they *wanted* to follow him through this story. And that helped make the film a hit. It was an important lesson that Goldman learned well. As I said you'll find plenty of magic moments in his scripts from then on out. (*Butch Cassidy and the Sundance Kid*, in particular, is filled with them—you can lose track trying to count them all.)

The Case of the Controversial Sports Bra

I myself learned the power of magic moments just from watching all those talk shows as a kid. Most nights they were pretty predictable. Guests would come out on their best behavior, and hosts would treat them respectfully. But on some nights ... the crazy happened, and I loved it. Like in the following:

- *Back to the Future* actor Crispin Glover almost kicked David Letterman in the head.

- Jay Leno confronted Hugh Grant after the actor was arrested when he was caught with a sex worker providing him with his own magic moment by asking, "What were you thinking?"

- Music legend Madonna let loose a nonstop stream of f-bombs aimed at a rattled Letterman.

I'm sure a lot of you readers recognize at least one or two of these famous or, in some cases, infamous talk show moments. I for one will never forget the Crispin Glover appearance. I was pretty young, and it was the first time I had seen a guest shot go haywire to the point where the host instantly went to commercial. When the break was over, Glover was nowhere to be found because Letterman had booted him from the show.

These moments live on long after they happened. Go to YouTube, just put the word "Crispin" in the search box, and "Glover Letterman" will quickly pop up after it as the most popular search term, even though this happened in 1987! But when it comes to real game changers, it's hard to beat the Jay Leno exchange with Hugh Grant. It's often cited as *the* episode that permanently turned the corner for Leno's popularity. After that night Letterman rarely beat him in the ratings despite having a much bigger audience up until then. Maybe he should have had Crispin Glover back on.

But there can also be a dark side to a magic moment, one that can ruin a career if it's bad enough. I'm sure many, if not most, of you remember when Tom Cruise went on *Oprah* and started jumping up and down on her couch. That crazy moment caused his audience to freak out as much as Tom appeared to be doing, and it took a while to build his career back up to its previous heights.

So let's learn a big lesson from Tom. You want to try to make your magic moments *positive*, ones that strike a chord with your audience instead of making them run for the exits. Put these kinds of moments to work for you, not against you. Those are the kinds of magic moments I still strive for to this day.

Here's one of my favorites from early in my radio years.

It was 1999, and the US Women's Soccer Team had just won the World Cup. What everyone remembers from that final was when player Brandi Chastain, after scoring the winning goal, spontaneously ripped off her jersey and fell to her knees, wearing only her sports bra above the waist. The photo of her celebrating was described by the *New York Times* as "the most iconic photograph ever taken of a female athlete."[5] While many applauded what she did, there was also a big backlash that chastised her for being inappropriate. So emotionally it was a little rough.

Still, it was a big deal, so big that New York City threw a parade for this talented team. After the parade the team made an appearance at a huge new Nike store that had just opened in midtown, Niketown. At that point I was still doing interviews outside the studio for the morning show, so it was natural that I'd want to go down and try to interview the players. But when I got there, it was a mob scene. Hundreds and hundreds of media people were surrounding Brandi

5   Jeré Longman, "The Sports Bra Seen Round the World Has New Meaning 20 Years Later," *New York Times*, July 5, 2019.

with their cameras, crews, and other equipment. Me? I was just this rando shlub with a microphone—competing with this media horde was going to be a real challenge.

At first I was intimidated. Then a funny thing happened. As I listened to all the other reporters' questions, they all seemed … well, a little lame. These women had just won a huge victory, but that wasn't the topic of the day. Instead these media hotshots wanted to stay focused on the sports bra controversy and hammer Brandi about what she did. It seemed very negative and oppressive. And that, I felt, gave me my opening.

So when it was finally my turn to talk to Brandi, the right question just popped into my head. "You know," I said to her, "everyone's talking about your jersey, but how's it going to feel when you walk down the street and you happen to see a little girl wearing a Brandi Chastain jersey of their own?"

My question caused Brandi to break down in tears. This woman who had just won the World Cup in front of a hundred million people was finally asked about the *positive* influence of her actions and how kids might actually be inspired by her. This turned out to be the "magic moment" all the press highlighted in their coverage. It couldn't go viral, not yet, not in 1999—internet usage wasn't that huge yet. But the moment was recognized, even if I wasn't. One article referred to me only as "a guy with a microphone," but the folks back at WPLJ knew who that guy was, so it raised my stock at the radio station.

Make Some Magic of Your Own

So yes, magic moments can manufacture some magic for careers such as mine, but they can also impact everyday conversations. For example, there are magic moments in job interviews when the candidate and the interviewer click in a meaningful way (and it could be over something as trivial as loving the same sports team). A business meeting can yield a magic moment when someone makes an observation that causes a rethink of a plan or goal. Breakthroughs in personal relationships can also frequently be traced to a magic moment that yielded an insight or revelation that caused one party to view the other from a completely new perspective.

For all these reasons and more, creating magic moments in conversations is a skill well worth developing. We usually view these kinds of things as "happy accidents," and most probably are, but the truth is, if we're truly engaged in our conversations at a high level, the odds are our magic moments will be far from accidental.

If we're truly engaged in our conversations at a high level, the odds are our magic moments will be far from accidental.

The rest of this book is devoted to giving you the tools and techniques you need to make magic moments happen, as well as good conversations in general. And one of the most important tips is spotlighted in the very next chapter. Here's a hint: it's something your mom probably told you never to do.

CHAPTER 3

THE SECRET TO CONVERSATIONAL SUCCESS
BE NOSY!

WHEN YOU WERE A CHILD, did you ever innocently ask someone a very personal question?

It's something that's happened to most of us because when you're growing up, you're just figuring out what's okay to ask and what's not. And you learn fast because when you do ask something that maybe goes too far, whatever authority figure that's lurking around (parent, teacher, older sibling, etc.) will quickly shush you. They'll tell you it's not your business. It's inappropriate. And then they drop the hammer and give you the rule you're not allowed to argue with, the one that gets burned into your brain and shuts down part of it.

"Don't be nosy."

Suddenly you feel restricted. You feel the need to be careful. And it ends up inhibiting your conversation for the rest of your life. Unless you're me. I am nosy and proud of it. That trait is really responsible for my whole career and has helped me do many a good interview. But I still get flak for it.

For instance, my wife and I were sitting around the pool of our building the other day, and our neighbor was sitting next to us. And because I am naturally curious, I suddenly launched into interview mode and began to ask him all these questions about himself while my wife grew more and more uncomfortable with what I was doing. Afterward she said to me, "Why are you so nosy?"

Well, again, to me, it's the secret of my success. It's why I dove into the depths of pop culture when I was growing up—I always wanted to know more about the movies and TV shows, as well as the actors who were in them, so I made it a mission to learn what I could. As mentioned in chapter 1, that's exactly how I earned my ticket into the radio studio—I was the trivia guy the other guys could rely on. (Now Google is the only "trivia guy" anybody needs.)

Here's my take on it. Being nosy doesn't have to be a bad thing. For me (and for you as an interviewer), it's mostly a good thing. Scott Shannon, my mentor, pegs it as one of the three most important qualities an on-air personality can have. (The other two are passion and a strong work ethic.) It pushes me to ask things other people won't and gets me places others don't get to go. And I find out a lot, even when I ask a question some may view as a little out of line. Most people aren't offended by a potentially invasive question if they feel you're on their side and your timing is right.

Why? Because of this little secret you may not know—most people *love* to talk about themselves. And as long as you're friendly and respectable when you're asking people personal questions, being nosy will more

> *As long as you're friendly and respectable when you're asking people personal questions, being nosy will more often than not get them to open up and tell you things they wouldn't otherwise share.*

often than not get them to open up and tell you things they wouldn't otherwise share.

So let's talk about how to be effectively nosy because when you are, you set the stage for great conversations.

When Jennifer Met Monkey Boy

The first step to being nosy? Lose your fear.

That can be hard. As detailed at the opening of this chapter, you're trained from childhood *not* to be too curious. (You were probably told multiple times that curiosity somehow is fatal to felines.) It's a societal norm you feel obliged to follow. But you have to fight that training to an extent. Yes, there definitely is a line you have to respect. The trick is to step up to it without crossing it. A lot of the time, that's the only way you even get *access* to someone you want to talk to.

Rockin' sexy USA attire on the streets of New York— a bit inspired by the "desnudas" scandal.

Here's an example. When I was just starting out with the morning show, Scott and Todd would frequently send me out on the street to get interviews, like at red-carpet events and such. I got a lot of great experience from those assignments. Anyway, one day somebody called into the station and tipped us off that Jennifer Aniston was filming a movie right across the street from our studios in Midtown Manhattan. So what did Scott and Todd do? They turned to me and said, "Go down there and interview Jennifer Aniston."

Oh. Okay.

While she's obviously still a big star today, at that time she was a huge phenomenon, starring on the number one show *Friends* (maybe you've heard of it?) and parlaying her TV success into a movie career. Plus apparently she used to be married to Brad Pitt? Yeah, pretty sure that happened. Anyway the point is she was a superstar, and I was Monkey Boy. A rando like me was going to get a one-on-one with her between setups on a movie set? I didn't think so. But it was my job, so I had to try. I swallowed my fear and went to where her trailer was parked on Thirty-Fourth Street between Seventh and Eighth Avenue. What was my game plan? Well, I didn't have much of one. Like an idiot, I decided to just go knock on her trailer door. I say "idiot" because between me and that door was a very, very, very large security guard who looked like he used to be an offensive tackle for the Dallas Cowboys. (Offensive linemen are known to be quite large, just so you know.)

Still, I didn't take him seriously. My thinking was, "Ah, what's the worst he can do? I'm just a tiny white guy who looks about as threatening as a roll of paper towels." But then he saw me and sensed what I was about to do. He made a beeline straight for me. My attitude quickly shifted to "Holy crap, he's going to kill me."

Holding up my radio mic, I said in my most soothing and innocent tone, "Hey, I only want to ask Jennifer a couple of questions, that's all." The guard let me know that wasn't going to happen. His tone was neither soothing nor innocent.

Then a weird thing happened—Jennifer, inside the trailer, heard what was going on. She stuck her head out and asked what was going on. So I introduced myself as Monkey Boy (always impressive) from 'PLJ radio. She told me she was sorry she couldn't talk right now and retreated back inside. All this seemed to make the security guy even angrier. He invaded my personal space and made it clear he was *not* f—ing sorry and I better leave. I took his sage advice and returned to the studio with my tail between my legs. I apologized to the crew for my failure.

But then another weird thing happened. A couple of minutes later, Jennifer Aniston had her assistant call the front desk at 'PLJ to say Jennifer felt badly about what happened. Better yet, she'd be happy to do an interview with the morning show. So they patched her through, and she talked for twenty minutes with us about the movie she was making, her time on *Friends*, everything you'd want to talk about with Jennifer Aniston. A lot of magic moments there.

You see, curiosity combined with fearlessness can be your friend. Just know that the huge and angry security guard never will be.

Emotional Curiosity

Curiosity and fearlessness—I'm not the only one who knows this combination works.

Early in his career, famed movie and TV producer Brian Grazer, who won an Oscar for *A Beautiful Mind* and was behind such groundbreaking series as *24* and *Arrested Development*, began to seek out what he called "curiosity conversations." He made a rule for himself—he had to meet one new person in the entertainment business every day and try to find out what made them tick. He was surprised to find out these people, whom he didn't even know, were very willing to talk about themselves and their work in surprising depth—*just because he asked.*

Then he started to think ... maybe big-time authorities in *other* fields would be willing to do the same thing. Over the next thirty-five years, he was ballsy enough to track down others he wanted to know more about and ask for an hour of their time for a conversation in order to broaden his perspective and get some insights beyond the insular world of show business.

So Grazer ended up sitting down with both Carl Sagan and Isaac Asimov. Two CIA directors. Activists and astronauts. The guy who invented the H-bomb. He even met with people he didn't really want to meet. People he was actually *scared* of. As Grazer wrote in his book, "The point was to follow my curiosity, and I ranged as widely as I could ... The goal for me is to learn something. The results have always been surprising, and the connections I've made from the curiosity conversations have cascaded through my life—and the movies we make—in the most unexpected ways ... Over time, I discovered that I'm curious in a particular sort of way. My strongest sense of curiosity is what I call emotional curiosity: I want to understand what makes people tick; I want to see if I can connect a person's attitude and personality with their work, with their challenges and accomplishments."[6]

I share Grazer's emotional curiosity, and I think it's essential to have that component in place in order to be a successful interviewer. It makes you nosy in a *good* way. And it motivates you to ask questions designed to inform, not embarrass.

And believe it or not, most people want you to ask those questions. Most people *want* you to be nosy because it shows you

---

6   Brian Grazer and Charles Fishman, *A Curious Mind: The Secret to a Bigger Life* (New York: Simon & Schuster, 2015).

actually *care* about who they are. They feel recognized and valued. No doubt, you've been involved in one-sided conversations, where the other person goes on and on until you wonder if they'd even notice if you just got up and walked away. You feel ignored and slighted, and in the future you avoid talking with them if you can.

It even happens in professional situations. Ever watch a ball game where the announcers are too busy talking about what they had for dinner the night before to point out an amazing play that's taking place on the field? Or watch a late-night talk show interview where the host is too busy trying to hustle laughs than learn about the person sitting on the couch? Even my hero David Letterman did that a lot in the beginning of his hosting career before he mastered the art of the interview.

Not everyone is born with the kind of emotional curiosity Grazer possesses. But that doesn't mean you can't develop it over time. The beginning of building that skill starts by using the interviewer's main tool—questions.

Ask and Ye Shall Receive

Like I said earlier, I'm far from a member of academia (although I'm sure I left my mark after two whole years at William Paterson College). However, I'm smart enough to listen to it. For example, at the Harvard Business School, they've been studying conversations for a long time, and that research brought them to a huge insight—*most people don't ask enough questions*. They found that one of the most common complaints made after a conversation, whether a formal interview or a first date, is "I wish they had asked me more questions."[7]

---

7   Alison Wood Brooks and Leslie K. John, "The Surprising Power of Questions," *Harvard Business Review*, May–June 2018 issue, https://hbr.org/2018/05/the-surprising-power-of-questions.

Why don't people ask more questions, even in a situation where it should be all about questions, like a job interview? Well, as noted, some people are just too wrapped up in their own heads to consider what's going on in the interviewee's head. Others just aren't curious enough. And sometimes they're just plain scared they'll ask a dumb question and be viewed as either thoughtless or incompetent. Or, horrors, just plain nosy. But the fact is *most people don't understand how important questions are to relationships*.

Research shows that the more questions you ask, the more likely the other person will like you and bond with you.[8] For instance, with speed daters, people were more willing to go on a second date with prospective partners who asked more questions. And not necessarily a lot more questions. Here's a wild fact from that study: Asking *just one more question* on a date helped persuade the other party to go out with them again. Asking questions, as I already noted, communicates to the other person that you value them and are interested in them. If someone is interested in us, we tend to view them more favorably. And it will cause us to open up a lot more because it builds a certain level of trust.

> **Asking questions, as I already noted, communicates to the other person that you value them and are interested in them.**

Questions work a lot better when they're in the right context. You don't ask a question for the sake of asking a question. You ask a question based on who you believe the person is and where the conversation is going. You want to show them you're not a threat and that you just want to understand who they are and what they're all about. They should get why you're asking the question you're

---

8   Ibid.

asking—it should have relevance to their persona and the conversation you're having. Otherwise it could be perceived as a "gotcha" question, a question that's designed to make them look bad.

Say, for example, I ask Jennifer Aniston out of the blue, "You ever kill anybody?" And let's say Jen, taken aback, stutters and stammers and sounds like maybe she's covering up a homicide. The clip goes viral. TMZ leads their show with "Did Jennifer Aniston murder someone? If so, who?" Well, guess what. Jen ain't coming out of her trailer for you after that!

Now I could see asking her security guard that question, but I could also see myself becoming his first victim as a result. That's a joke, but seriously it's a question that *could* come up with someone in security or law enforcement if the conversation brings you to that place. They do the type of work where that could actually happen. But again, you have to be in a moment where that question is justified, like if the person is talking about the dangerous and violent situations they have had to face in the past. It's not justified if you're talking to someone who was famous for getting into zany escapades with Chandler, Joey, Ross, Phoebe, and Monica.

Finding the right context for a question is much easier when you develop emotional curiosity. You're able to read signals the other person is putting out, what they'd be open to talking about, and what they absolutely don't want to talk about. You connect on a deeper level, and that pays off in the back-and-forth that you're able to create through asking the right questions. Be sympathetic and supportive and you'll be surprised at what people will share.

Let me return to academia one more time (I got a day pass) to prove what I'm saying here. Todd Kashdan, who did a study on curiosity at George Mason University, said of his findings, "Being interested is more important in cultivating a relationship and maintaining a relationship than being interesting; that's what gets the dialogue going. It's the secret juice of relationships."[9]

FOUR WAYS TO ASK THE RIGHT QUESTIONS

When you're doing podcasts, you will frequently talk with someone you don't know that well—or at all. This is where asking the right questions can be critical. The wrong ones can put the other person on the defensive and cause them to withdraw rather than share. With that in mind, here are four ways to approach questions that will create trust and bonding rather than distrust and suspicion:

1. Choose positive questions, especially at first. Avoid anything that might trigger a negative reaction and you'll get off on the right foot.

2. Focus on open-ended questions that can motivate a great story. For example, ask if there was something in their past that brought them to the place they are in life. If you only ask specifics, you risk getting one-word yes and no answers that don't shine a light on who this person really is.

3. Make the other person feel important. You don't have to kiss up to someone to do that. You make them feel valued just by showing genuine interest in them and what they have to say.

---

9   Jill Suttie, "Why Curious People Have Better Relationships," *Greater Good Magazine*, May 31, 2017, https://greatergood.berkeley.edu/article/item/why_curious_people_have_better_relationships?utm_source=Greater+Good+Science+Center&utm_campaign=694ab4495d-GG_EMAIL_CAMPAIGN_2017_05_24&utm_medium=email&utm_term=0_5ae73e326e-694ab4495d-50942075.

4. Choose questions that drive a conversation. Your questions should help set a mood, establish rapport, and build to magical moments.

Curious and Curiouser

You never know what you might find out from asking a question. But here's what you'll find out if you don't ask: absolutely nothing. When you're in the middle of a conversation, you may be struck by something odd the other person says or does and not know whether you should react to it. In most cases I want to find out what's going on. It may not be much, but sometimes you get a game-changing answer. That's a gift, but you only get that gift if you go after it. And to end this chapter, let me share a prime example of that.

Singer-songwriter John Mayer was a friend of our radio show, and he, along with other music stars, would perform at a Christmas show we would put on for kids at Blythedale Children's Hospital, a long-term children's medical facility that was world-renowned for its good works. Usually I would get on stage with John and our other guests before the shows to warm them up and map out how everything was going to go.

Well, one year John said he wanted to perform a Christmas song. He took out a piece of hotel stationery with the lyrics of Mariah Carey's "All I Want for Christmas Is You" handwritten on it.

On stage with John Mayer for the annual 95.5 'PLJ Christmas show at Blythedale Children's Hospital.

I looked at those handwritten lyrics. And I was struck by one thing, and yes, I know we're not supposed to gender things these days, but the lyrics looked like they were written by a woman. And that made me curious. So I flat-out asked, "Who wrote out those lyrics? It doesn't look like you did it."

John smiled and said, "My girlfriend and I stayed up late at my hotel, and she wrote them down." And I smiled. Because I knew who his girlfriend was at that time.

Yep, Jennifer Aniston.

"Hey, that's awesome!" I said. "Do you guys mind if we auction these lyrics off and give the money to the children's hospital?" John quickly agreed. He knew it was a great idea. And so did Scott and Todd when I told them about it. As a matter of fact, they were blown away, and it was another feather in my cap at the time. Best of all, the auction of that piece of hotel stationery ended up raising about $5,000 for the hospital.

Now my thinking could have been "Well, who actually wrote down those song lyrics is none of my business. I should keep my yap shut." Well, regrets, I have a few, but asking that question is definitely not one of them. The handwriting stood out to me, and I really wanted to know whose it was.

All of us sometimes get stuck in our own heads. When that happens, we don't take the time to really observe what's going on around us or with the other person. We're not *present*. And we miss out on a lot of opportunities as a result. Successful interactions happen when you focus on the other person, not yourself. You have to let go of your own ego and figure out what the other person is trying to say.

It also helps if Jennifer Aniston is somehow involved ...

CHAPTER 4

IF YOU'RE DOING MORE TALKING THAN LISTENING, YOU'RE DOING IT WRONG

A FEW YEARS AGO, Chris Martin from Coldplay was scheduled to come to our studio in the afternoon. We were going to interview him after the morning show was over, record it, and play parts of it on the next morning show. He was also going to perform a song.

A little while before he was due to arrive, his roadie came in and set up about twelve guitars and two pianos, all for what was supposedly going to be one song. It took him four hours just to get the stuff up there using the freight elevator. I asked the roadie, "Why all this for one number?" The roadie shrugged. "I have to prepare for anything. I don't know what kind of mood he'll be in."

Now that's the kind of sentence that can make an interviewer like me a little nervous. No matter what the media would have you believe, celebrities are people like anyone else, and yes, they might enter in a lighthearted mood and open to joking around, but they could also walk in with a black cloud swirling around them that's determined to make themselves and everyone around them miserable (see Russell Crowe, chapter 10).

Fortunately Chris showed up with a smile. We already had a keyboard of our own in the studio for any guest who might want to play. Chris spotted it, walked right past the several billion instruments his roadie had brought in, looked down at it, and said, "All right, this'll do." He never touched the other instruments. Nor did he bother with a soundcheck or anything like that. He just got down to business without any hesitation. And then we started talking.

The interview went great. At one point he was telling a story about something that happened to him, and almost as a throwaway, he said, "I was making peanut butter and jelly sandwiches for the kids at the time ..."

I said, "Hold on a second," and stopped him in his tracks. Chris had been, of course, married to Gwyneth Paltrow, who was famous for her strict healthy-eating ways. However, this was after the twosome had, in Gwyneth's words, "consciously uncoupled." So I wanted to hear more about these sandwiches. "You just feed the kids peanut butter and jelly?"

He was a little taken aback. "What do you expect kids to eat?"

I responded, "I thought maybe you'd be giving them avocado jam and kale butter or something."

"No." He smiled, shaking his head. "My kids are regular kids. And I make them PBJ sandwiches."

It was a sweet magic moment that really humanized Chris for the audience and gave them a little peek into his personal life. But this moment would never have happened if I wasn't *listening* and focused on what he was saying. If I had been doggedly running down a list of questions I wanted to ask him, I probably would have blown right past that little aside and gone on to the next one.

Even though it seems as though it doesn't require much effort, doing the right kind of listening is *the* key element in an interviewer's toolbox. So that's what we're going to talk about in this chapter—because there's more to listening than you might think. So … listen up and read on!

The Joy of Zipping Your Lip

You might be surprised to learn that listening is our primary communication skill as human beings. According to one study, we spend about 9 percent writing, 16 percent reading, 30 percent speaking, and 45 percent listening.[10] Yeah. Almost half the time, we're just listening to others. And since we do that more than anything, you'd think we'd be pretty good at it, right?

Nope. Not at all.

Most people only retain about 50 percent of what they hear. And within forty-eight hours, that drops to 25 percent.[11] So we're actually pretty inefficient listeners, and we miss out on a lot that way. Now sometimes, I get it, someone's just going on about something we don't care about in a conversation that's no big deal, and we just zone out. You do it, I do it, everyone does it. But if you have to have an important personal or professional talk with someone, or if you interview people for a living, zoning out is *not* an option. Because that's how conversations lose momentum and drift away into the ether. It's also how you miss important cues and even crucial information.

Even though it seems as though it doesn't require much effort, doing the right kind of listening is the key element in an interviewer's toolbox.

---

10 Dick Lee and Delmar Hatesohl, "Listening: Our Most Used Communications Skill," University of Missouri Extension, October 1993, https://mospace.umsystem.edu/xmlui/bitstream/handle/10355/50293/cm0150-1993.pdf?sequence=1&isAllowed=y.

11 Ibid.

Todd Pettengill, one of my radio mentors I mentioned earlier, remembered when he learned how important listening is as a kid:

> For me, it started when I was probably seven or eight years old. I was in my church choir, and our choir director was kind of a hard ass. And we'd be goofing during practice, and he said, "Look, if God wanted you to talk more than he wanted you to listen, he'd have given you two mouths and one ear." And for some reason, that just stuck with me, so when I started in radio, that was always my approach. I mean, if you're not listening, then you're not able to react. Right? If you're not listening, you're missing half of the conversation. So you're only participating in half of the conversation if you're asking questions. If you're not listening to the responses, what are you doing? Anything? Because comedy and content lives everywhere if you listen for it. If you're only worried about getting in your next question, then it doesn't work. Your focus has to be on the subject. It always has to be. I've done interviews where I've asked one question, and then the rest of the interview is just listening, reacting, and responding to what the person says. To me, that's the best kind of interview.

I couldn't agree more. But as I said listening is a skill, and as with most skills, people have to work to get better at it. With listening, however, most don't believe it requires any real effort. It's kind of like breathing and smelling—we just do it. We've been hearing stuff since we were born, so we think we've mastered it. Well, in a way we have. We understand words and noises and what they signify. Good for us. But if we're interested in having more productive conversations or memorable interviews, well, we have to take listening to the next level.

First, recognize that there are two types of listening: active and passive. The default for most of us is passive listening. We go through our day focused on what we need to do and only listen closely when we have to or want to, like when somebody gives us instructions on something (a "have to") or there's a song that comes on that we love (a "want to"). Makes sense, right? Unfortunately we also tend to apply those same rules to our everyday conversations. Unless there's a "have to" or a "want to" factor attached to what the other person is saying, then we tend to tune out and just focus on what we want out of the conversation. (I don't know if you're aware, but humans can occasionally be *very* selfish.) When we approach an interaction thinking more about us than anything else, it can result in some interesting non sequiturs as well as some hurt feelings. For instance,

Person You're Talking To: It's been the *worst*. In the last two weeks, I've lost my car, my job, *and* my boyfriend.

Person Who's Not Listening: Hey, did you ever get a chance to check out the TikTok I posted? I rap and everything!

I think you can see how that talk isn't going to end well.

There's a guy I love who specializes in listening, and his name is William Ury. He's an expert negotiator (and best-selling author—his book *Getting to Yes* has sold twelve million copies) who's helped a lot of huge government leaders resolve conflicts. To do that he *had* to be a good listener; otherwise he might have missed a couple of words, and World War III might've broken out. Anyway he has a great take on the subject that sounds a lot like the advice from Todd's choir director: "We're given two ears and one mouth for a reason, to listen twice as much, at least, as we speak." So that's where he's coming from.

Ury has a very insightful short talk on "The Power of Listening" on YouTube,[12] where he lists the following three reasons why active listening makes our relationships easier:

---

12   "The Power of Listening, William Ury," TEDx Talks, YouTube, January 7, 2015, https://www.youtube.com/watch?v=saXfavo1OQo.

1. It helps us understand the other side.

The more you listen to someone, the more you'll see where they're coming from. This is especially helpful if the two of you are in the middle of some disagreement. If you start that kind of conversation by going after the other person, they're instantly going to get defensive. There will be a wall up because they think all you want to do is attack them, so you've guaranteed a bad beginning and possibly an outcome to match. If you do approach someone you've got a beef with, it's much better to let them talk first in an open and nonjudgmental manner. They'll feel free to share more, and you'll get a better sense of where they're coming from.

2. It helps us connect with the other person.

When you listen closely and react to what they're saying in the moment, they feel like you're with them and you two are a team. You build a rapport and you build trust because you're showing you *care*. Everyone wants to be heard, it's a basic human need, and when you meet that need, you create a bond. You also get a sense of how they use body language and other nonverbal cues to communicate and, in the process, gain a deeper understanding of the person.

3. It makes the other person more likely to listen to us.

If you're trying to influence the other person to make a good decision that they might be resisting, sometimes the best thing you can do is just sit back and let them vent before getting too far into it. Then when they're done exploding, they've gotten it out of their system, and odds are they will often be open to doing what you're asking … *as long as you don't keep arguing with them*. Frustration and anger sometimes have to be released before a serious discussion can be had.

Active listening is crucial to our work and our lives, even if you don't interview people for a living like I do. If you ignore or mishear an important work guideline, you can easily screw something up and have no one to blame but yourself. The same goes if your spouse calls you to tell you something important like the sump pump blew up and you just "mm-hmm" them on the phone while you scroll through Twitter. You'll come home to a backyard literally full of crap and wonder how it got there.

We take listening for granted. It's easy and it's natural. But real listening, active listening, is something that you need to learn and practice every day. And that means losing your own agenda as often as possible.

Check Your Ego at Your Mouth

Here's the big problem that crops up when we're listening to someone else talk. We usually start thinking, "How does this affect *me*? What do I agree with? What do I disagree with? What am I going to say next? And when do I get to say it?" In other words we keep our thoughts fixated on ourselves, even when we're not saying anything. And many of us are just impatiently waiting for our chance to jump in and take over.

Genuine active listening is just the opposite. We want to listen carefully to what the other person is trying to communicate. We try to empathize and put ourselves in their shoes. We try to get on their wavelength, not continue to listen to our own mental broadcasts. And we try to get beyond the person's words to "hear" what's going on underneath them. What kinds of emotions are they feeling? What does this person really need or want? What are they all about?

To meet that challenge, we have to train ourselves to do the following:

- ### *Don't judge!*

I mentioned Twitter a little earlier. If you've ever used it, you know judgment runs rampant. Someone posts an opinion about a song or a TV show and suddenly everyone is tearing them to shreds over something that usually ain't all that important. It's not your job to judge everyone else's thoughts, and honestly all it does is put up barriers between you and others.

- ### *Shhhh.*

Often people get anxious when a moment of silence comes in a conversation. But sometimes that moment is important. It gives both people a chance to consider what's being discussed before they speak again. But silence can really freak people out—they end up rushing to fill the space with words that don't add anything. There's a better way, especially if you're interviewing someone as a professional and can't risk a dead spot: Ask open-ended questions like "So what do you think?" or "What happened after that?" to keep the dialogue going.

- ### *Restate and sum up.*

It can be powerful for you to acknowledge what the other person is expressing and paraphrase it so they see you understand (or at least are trying to understand) what they're communicating. Start with "So what you're saying is …" and repeat, using your own words, what the other person said. That demonstrates you have been listening and get the gist of it. The person can also clarify if you're getting it wrong, and by the way it's okay if you are getting it wrong. What matters is you're showing you care enough to get it right.

- ### *Follow up with questions.*

When someone is telling you a story, say, about a car accident they had, try to resist the urge to immediately talk about when you had a car accident three years ago. They may not be done talking about their experience, so give them the chance and follow up with questions that allow them to provide more context and allow you to understand any underlying issues. You demonstrate genuine curiosity or concern when you ask questions about what they're talking about, and that, in turn, makes them trust you more. And show empathy. Say things like "I imagine how hard that must have been," if they just made it through something difficult, or "Wow, you must be over the moon," if there's happy news.

• ***Pay attention to what they don't say.***

People don't just communicate with words. If someone, for example, sighs or rolls their eyes in the middle of a story, comment on those behaviors. "What's wrong?" "You seem upset." Or if they're almost dancing while they're talking, "So this is good?" Nonverbal cues and body language can tell you a lot if you pay attention to it.

By the way if you're rolling your eyes at all this—"This dude thinks I have to learn to listen?"—I get it. But at the same time, I know that training yourself to listen actively is essential to creating great, productive conversations. And all you have to do is lose your ego and give the spotlight to the speaker. My take is this: Hey, if I want to hear myself talk, I might as well do it to the bathroom mirror on my own time. I talk to other people to hear what *they* have to say, not me. Now obviously I'm not going to put myself completely on mute during a conversation. No, I'll speak up, either to ask a question, answer a question that's put to me, add a relevant comment, or tell a story that contributes to what we're talking about. But I'm not going to go in with a secret agenda to make the interaction work the way I want it to.

Training yourself to listen actively is essential to creating great, productive conversations.

That's especially true when I'm hosting a show or interviewing people. I've found that trying to map out a conversation in advance just never works. When you do that, you strip away all spontaneity and potential for surprises because all you're doing is running through a bucket list of your own making. With that in mind, I never make a numbered list of questions that I want to ask a guest. This might just be me, but I find the mathematics part of my brain (yes, I have one) kicks in and compels me to ask them in the order I numbered them. I'm focused on asking the questions I want to ask in the order I want to ask them instead of focused on what the other person is saying.

A true conversation doesn't go in a planned and linear direction. A true conversation has tangents and detours and unexpected jumps and callbacks. That's what makes talk interesting and sometimes unforgettable. (I'll give you another good example of that in a moment.) What would have been my question number one would probably never be followed by my question number two in a real conversation. Instead the answer to question number one might prompt me to ask next question number eight or nine and question number four, and I have to let that happen. Otherwise the exchanges end up stilted and choppy because there's no natural flow, the kind of flow that takes you to unexpected, fun, and/or emotional destinations. So when I write up some questions in advance, I just bullet point them and use them as a reference point, not as a blueprint.

I have a very tall and very bald Australian friend named Brad Blanks who used to do red-carpet interviews for us at WPLJ (after I finally graduated from those kinds of assignments and got to stay in the studio). Brad actually still does the same thing for my old boss Scott Shannon, who's now a morning host at WCBS in New York. The last time I spoke to Brad, I wanted to get his thoughts on interviewing. Here's what he had to say:

You can push too much if you expect the interview to go a certain way. If you push too much, then I don't want to say you'll fail, but it won't come out how you want it to. I think as I've evolved and gotten older, I have to aim for the good interviews and hope that my natural style will get an odd laugh here and there. And not for me. I'm always aiming for the person I'm interviewing to provide the laughs. And hopefully that sort of becomes teamwork in the interview; I'm setting it up for them.

When you're going with a plan into these interviews, that can be the worst thing. Yes, you need a sketch of where you want it to go and maybe even think of an opening question or two designed to build that rapport. You want those rapport-building questions as quickly as possible because you want to create a bond quickly. You want them to be on your team and play your game. And that can be troubling if you've overprepared because you're too busy thinking of the questions in your head that you're going to go to. And in my case I'm sitting there going, all right, I have the three or four points that I want to hear, but what I'm asking now is more important if I can jump on an interesting tangent and follow up on it.

I agree 100 percent with everything Brad says. Active listening helps you go with the other person's flow and discover things you don't know. It also frequently opens up amazing new areas of discussion.

Here's an example of that that I hinted at earlier.

When I was doing my *Science of Sex* podcast, we did an episode where we interviewed a young woman from Las Vegas who was working toward her PhD by doing a study of sex workers—how they lived their lives, how it affected them emotionally and physically, and so forth. She revealed to us she always wanted to understand more about this world, most of which takes place in the shadows, so she went for it. How? Well, one of the first things she did was approach the owner of a brothel in Nevada, a state where prostitution is legal in some areas. And she said to him, "Listen, I want to study sex workers for my doctorate. It's not to attack them but to support them and find out more about their lives." The owner listened to her pitch and then said, "Absolutely, you can have access to all of my girls." She was over the moon and quickly responded, "Great!" But then he said, "Well, there's one stipulation ... You have to work here."

Now imagine if I was busy thinking about my next question and let that remark just hang there. Imagine if I just rolled past it and went on to a different part of her experience. Imagine if I just shrugged to myself and assumed she was going to work the front desk or something. If you can imagine all that, you can also imagine I shouldn't be doing what I do. I mean ... *whoa*. It turned out that this woman actually became a sex worker to study sex workers! And that was definitely an experience worth exploring—it helped make this episode one of my all-time favorites.

Whether it's what Chris Martin makes his kids for lunch or what some people will do to get their doctorate, listening unlocks the kinds of magic moments that you always want to create in a conversation. And in the next chapter, we'll explore yet another way to make them happen. This time it's something Mom would approve of ... sharing!

CHAPTER 5

SHARING IS CARING
OPEN UP AND THE OTHER PERSON WILL TOO

AUTHOR TRUMAN CAPOTE ONCE SAID, "A conversation is a dialogue, not a monologue." Now I'm not an expert on Capote, but I found this quote on the internet, so it must be true, right? Well, even if it's not, the thought expressed in those words is totally valid.

The fact that a conversation is a back-and-forth proposition may seem obvious. But unfortunately for many people, it's not. These folks don't see another person on the other side of a talk. No, they only see a giant ear that God apparently sent to listen to every single thing they have to say. In other words they *want* it to be a monologue, their monologue, not a dialogue. And if that's what they're interested in doing, they should book an off-off-off-Broadway theater (maybe one in Paramus) and take to the stage every night to share their thoughts.

This is how I look at it: a good conversation is a bicycle. Note that I didn't say *riding* a bicycle … I meant it actually *is* a bicycle.

Here's why. A bicycle runs on two wheels. And you need both of those wheels to move forward, right? I mean, if the front tire locks up, you'll go flying over the handlebars. If the back tire goes flat, you'll have a hard time getting anywhere. And if you just get off the bike, the wheels, of course, stop moving altogether, and the whole thing flops over on its side.

Well, that's what a conversation is like. You and the other person are the wheels; you both have to keep the bike moving down the street, or the whole dialogue will collapse just like a real bike. You don't want that, so in this chapter let's talk about how to stop it from happening by uncovering another huge key to keeping a conversation upright and rolling onward and upward.

That key is *sharing*.

The More You Give, the More You Get

I have a wonderful niece named Kaitlyn. She's all grown up now, but when she was a kid, she was, to be honest, a little selfish.

Of course almost every kid is. They all want to hang on to whatever they have in hand until the apocalypse or bedtime, whichever comes first. Kaitlyn was no different. So her parents and I always had to remind her, "Remember, Kaitlyn, sharing is caring. *Sharing is caring*." To the point where the phrase is burned into my brain for all eternity.

But I'm not complaining. "Sharing is caring" is an idea I always want to keep front and center when I do interviews. Because sharing is not only caring, but it's also a way to inspire the other person to tell you something they might otherwise hold back. That deepens a conversation, which makes those two bicycle wheels really start rolling.

Here's an example of what I'm talking about. Jessie James Decker, if you haven't heard of her, is a singer, actor, and reality show star. In 2013 she married Eric Decker, who was a wide receiver for the Broncos at the time. By the time I interviewed her in 2014, however, Eric had been signed as a free agent by the Jets (shudder). Why would someone willingly sign with this less-than-stellar team? I would say the $36 million contract the Jets offered might have been a little bit of an incentive.

Although Jessie was in our studio to talk about her new album, I wanted to ask her about how her husband felt about his new team because I was and am a Jets fan, and the Jets were just horrible that season. Feel free to replace "that" with "every" (except for maybe 1968, you know, before I was born).

Sharing is not only caring, but it's also a way to inspire the other person to tell you something they might otherwise hold back.

Now this was a potentially touchy subject. So I had to be careful how I got into it. I said to her, "You know, Jessie, it's hard to be a Jets fan. We lose all the time. It's depressing. What's it like for Eric as a player?"

I got a shocking answer. She said, "It's been a really hard season. He's been, I don't want to say depressed, but he's been depressed. He has been. It's been really hard, and my heart breaks for him." She went on to say that after the team lost, Eric came home and just wanted to be alone. "He says, 'Don't talk to me.'"[13]

Now, again, people involved in pro sports (or, in Jessie's case, pro sports–adjacent) usually don't admit such things. And I don't think she would have if I hadn't first shared my own pain at following the team. I showed my concern for them, and she responded in kind. And because I led with empathy, she didn't feel threatened and didn't shut me down. (By the way the Deckers are still married and have three

---

13   Justin Tasch, "Jessie James Decker Says Eric Decker Is 'Depressed' over NY Jets Losses," *Daily News*, December 2, 2014, https://www.nydailynews.com/sports/football/jets/eric-decker-depressed-losses-wife-article-1.2029817.

kids, so don't worry, I didn't inspire a divorce.) To my surprise the interview went viral, popping up on TMZ and countless other media outlets. I guess I shouldn't be surprised because, as I said, pro sports people usually don't say things like that when there's a microphone in the vicinity.

Here's my point. When you share your own feelings and experiences, you remove barriers to having a deep and meaningful conversation. Of course this only works if you do the kind of active listening we discussed in chapter 3. That active listening can actually give you clues on a line of conversation you might want to pursue later on. It also allows you to find places where you can bond. For example, if someone hints at a situation that bugs them, and it's a situation that bugs you too, bring it up in the context of your own feelings about it. They're likely to open up about the problem, as Jessie James Decker did with me. Whatever the case, if you're coming from an authentic place, the other person can feel that … and is often excited to connect on a deeper level.

By the way there are also *nonverbal* ways to open up to another person—body language sometimes speaks louder than words, as I'm about to illustrate.

Kneel before Arnold!

What do you do if Arnold Schwarzenegger kind of hates you?

My friend Brad Blanks, who I introduced in the last chapter, encountered Arnold very early in his career. As I mentioned Brad is a very, very, very tall Australian who has made a career out of doing red-carpet interviews. But his height, especially in the beginning, was a problem. It either scared celebrities or … well, I'll let Brad tell this story. Look for another cameo appearance by our old friend Jennifer Aniston.

I'm big. I look like an ex-college linebacker. People would see me and go, "Oh, look at this wanker. What's he going to do to me here?" So before a famous person would get to me, I would have to befriend their publicist or manager and let them know their client was going to be in a safe space with me and that I wouldn't disrespect them. I also used a softer voice than my normal one to indicate this was going to be okay. Like a doctor's voice when they talk to kids to calm them down right before they give them a shot.

But I can't really do anything about my height. One time at the premiere of an Adam Sandler and Jennifer Aniston movie, I was literally on my knees on the ground, surrounded in a media scrum. Jennifer spots me and asks me to stand up. And when I did they immediately saw I was about two feet taller than either of them. And it scared the absolute shit out of them.

Now I love Arnold Schwarzenegger. I grew up watching his movies, so when he was at an event I was covering, I was excited. And suddenly there he was, right in front of me.

I swear I think I was at least a foot taller than the guy. And he was not happy about that. I quickly caught that. So I bent my knees and dropped my body, and by the end of that two-minute interview, I was half a foot smaller than him. The smaller I made myself, the better the interview got. It turned out to be a great talk. If you're dealing with big egos and you want to get something out of them, that is the kind of thing you have to do.

Yep, Brad got the interview and was lucky not to get scoliosis in the process. But you have to sacrifice for your art, right?

Part of the whole "sharing is caring" scenario is recognizing you may be doing something that makes the other person uncomfortable, something that has nothing to do with what you're saying but what you're *doing*. For instance, if you're standing there with your arms crossed and your head tilted back away from the other person, they're going to feel shut out, even though you had no intention of communicating that idea. Result? They may not open up to you just because, on some primal level, they don't feel you're truly trying to reach out. But when you change up your body language, make it more welcoming and friendlier, you remove another barrier to connecting.

Most people think looking at someone's face is the best way to discover what that person is feeling. Not true. The truth is body language is much more powerful in terms of communicating what you feel. Your facial expressions can be ambiguous and tough to read, especially if you're trying to suppress what you feel. Body language usually doesn't lie, which is why you have to be conscious of your posture and physicality when you're talking in person to someone.[14] It's a science Brad has mastered out of necessity because he's so tall he scares people. You too may have to adjust what you're doing with your body language to make others feel comfortable talking to you.

But please only resort to kneeling if it's Arnold. I mean, you kind of have to because even at his age, he could probably still kick the shit out of you.

---

14   Morgan Kelly, "Don't Read My Lips! Body Language Trumps the Face for Conveying Intense Emotions," Princeton University Office of Communication, January 15, 2013, https://www.princeton.edu/news/2013/01/15/dont-read-my-lips-body-language-trumps-face-conveying-intense-emotions.

Opening Up Both Sides of a Conversation

I want to make it clear that this isn't about "tricking" someone into telling you something they don't want to tell you. I wasn't out to blindside Jessie James Decker with my Jets question; I was genuinely interested in the answer as a Jets fan, and I think she picked up on that fact.

No, sharing is caring is about creating a quality conversation that hopefully can result in a deeper understanding of each other. We've all seen, heard, or read perfunctory interviews where a person sits down with a prepared list of questions and just asks them one after another, with little follow-up and no real attempt at making a connection. You don't get much out of listening to those, except maybe a few pieces of hard information you could have gotten through googling.

No, this is about creating an intimate conversation that works on a human level. And to do that you must first establish trust so the other person feels it's okay to disclose something a little personal. That trust can be built by sharing your own feelings about something that the other person also cares about. When you do that and you keep it 100 percent, it activates their empathy and creates the kind of bond that gets past all the superficial crap people usually talk about. It can also take both of you into areas where you can actually learn from each other and compare experiences. It gives *value* to the conversation, the kind of value that's missing from, say, an extensive discussion of the weather or what happened on *Succession* the previous night.

And let's remember there are times where it's *crucial* to get someone to open up. Think about a job interview or a college interview. If you're vetting someone for whatever reason, you want to dig a little to find out what the other person is really about. It's also important when you're considering starting a new relationship and want to know more about that potential significant someone before you get in any deeper. You can also make some hefty deposits in your knowledge bank by talking to strangers and asking questions (like me, Mr. Nosy). It's a great way to learn about different people's experiences and cultures and walk away with a broader understanding of the world. You can even get valuable advice if it's someone who knows how to handle an issue you're wrestling with.

So practically speaking, how do you do sharing and caring? Well, here are a few tips from *Psychology Today* that sum up what I'm talking about in this chapter:[15]

1. Remember the aforementioned active listening.

If you've trained yourself in active listening, this is something you'll do naturally when you talk to someone. If you haven't, it's not brain surgery or advanced calculus—all you have to do is just pay attention to what the other person is sharing as you begin to talk. It can give you the cues you need as to where to take the conversation. Look for something unusual or interesting about the person that you feel the urge to ask about.

2. Look for points of connection.

Are you both waiting in a line that's too long? Maybe you're both from the same part of the country? Or could be you've both served time for grand larceny (small world!). As you're talking, create a little Venn diagram in your head as to where you and the other person overlap in your life experiences and work off that connection to create a bond. Like maybe both of you are depressed once again about how badly the Jets suck this season.

---

15   Susan Krauss Whitbourne PhD, "5 Tips for Getting Anyone to Open Up," *Psychology Today*, February 11, 2017 https://www.psychologytoday.com/us/blog/fulfillment-any-age/201702/5-tips-getting-anyone-open.

3. Don't assume or you make an ass out of you and me.

Howard Hughes was the richest man in the world at one time, and still he traveled around in dirty tennis shoes, dirty clothes, dirty everything. Nobody would have guessed this guy had millions to burn. On the other hand, someone might dress to the nines and be flat broke at the moment. Before you make a snap judgment about someone, get to know them a little first. You may be surprised. I frequently am.

4. Ask questions from a friendly and respectful perspective.

As I said in chapter 3, being nosy is an asset to a conversation. Being a jerk, however, isn't. Getting too personal too fast is going to make people back away, not go deep with you. Start with general questions and follow their lead as to when to get more specific. If they're uncomfortable, apologize and find something else to talk about, which brings us to tip number five …

5. Know when to move forward and when to shift into reverse.

When you hit a great topic that excites both of you, step on the gas and drive on. But sometimes those topics don't come up, and sometimes the other person just isn't interested in being forthcoming. With a personal talk, that's okay—be polite and say your goodbyes. When you're doing an interview in a professional context, however, it gets a little trickier because you have to get through the thing. (We'll talk about this in a later chapter, but generally there are ways to keep the talk flowing well enough so that things turn out okay.) Generally the other person will warn you away from something they don't want to talk about by, for example, stonewalling or giving you a look that says, "Back off, Charlie" (or whatever your name happens to be). As that wise old philosopher Kenny Rogers used to say, "You got to know when to hold 'em, know when to fold 'em."

Anyway it's time to fold 'em on this chapter. Come to think of it, we're about halfway through this book, and I think you're due for some comic relief. Well, that's what I'll be delivering in the next chapter. I will admit that sadly I am out of Jennifer Aniston stories, but I think you'll still enjoy what's to come.

CHAPTER 6

"YES, AND ..."

THE IMPROV COMEDY CONCEPTS THAT KEEP CONVERSATION FLOWING

HERE'S A FUNNY THING about conversation: I got better at it after I began taking improv comedy classes.

Now your next question might be ... why did I enter into the improv world?

Well, as I've mentioned already, I was always a big fan of talk shows. But what I didn't mention was my passion for sketch comedy too. I grew up watching legends like Eddie Murphy on *Saturday Night Live* (*SNL*), and I loved the vibe, which made me always want to try some live performing on my own. And after I had been doing radio for a few years, I felt the need to perform with an actual audience in front of me. In the radio studio, all I had was the rest of the morning team to respond to my jokes, and I was feeling the need to break out beyond the soundproof room that was my professional home. But I knew I couldn't just pop up on a stage somewhere without the right training.

Luckily for me, in the late '90s, the Upright Citizens Brigade (UCB, born in Chicago and founded by such future *SNL* stars as Amy Poehler and Horatio Sanz) relocated to NYC and began offering classes. They had a four-level curriculum that included Improv 101, 201, 301, and 401, and I decided to go all in, so far in that I completed all four levels in one year!

So I got my comedy chops. And I got something else out of the classes that I had honestly never anticipated happening—I found I could directly apply some of the concepts they taught me to my day job at 'PLJ. The classes helped me become better at interviews, so much better that I thought it was important to share what I learned there in this book.

Performing with my sketch comedy group, Clip Show, at The People's Improv and UCB Theatre

Just Say No to No

There is perhaps no more important idea in improv than "Yes, and ..." It's such an important idea that it's now used in business training, which is no laughing matter. It's even been spotlighted in *Forbes* magazine.[16]

How does it work? Well, let's say you're on stage with your improv partner and you start out by stating you're a brain surgeon. But your partner instantly exclaims with disdain, "No, you're not!" Instant derailment. You're left standing there with egg on your face, facing a confused audience. The premise you put out there has been yanked out from under you, leaving you wondering what to do next and what your "partner" might do to you next.

That's a big improv no-no because your partner should always *support* what you're doing instead of short-circuiting it. In the improv situation I just described, the partner should have given a "Yes, and ..." response that indicated you were indeed a brain surgeon and you could move on to the next step of that premise. All they had to say was something like "Oh, you are? Tell me more." That way, you're working together, building on that simple premise and seeing where it leads.

It's no different with a conversation or interview—it should be something that's being constructed by the two of you rather than a game of Jenga where one of you could at any moment trigger a complete collapse. Here's how the UCB puts it: "Starting ... with agreement is like building the basement of a house. It's never the most decorative part of the structure, but the basement is certainly the sturdiest. It holds the essential materials to make the rest of the

---

16   Jennifer Oleniczak Brown, "Leading with a 'Yes, And,'" *Forbes*, April 6, 2017, https://www.forbes.com/sites/forbescoachescouncil/2017/04/06/leading-with-a-yes-and/?sh=3522b680588e.

house function, and it must support all the weight you build on top of it."[17]

Now let me dispose of one misconception you might have about "Yes, and ..." It doesn't necessarily mean you're *agreeing* with the person. It's more like "Yes, I accept what you're telling me, and here's more information I have to add." That new information is what keeps the conversation flowing. As another excerpt from the UCB Manual states, "When we speak to people in real life, we move the conversation forward by adding new information in response to what has already been communicated. Imagine that you are talking with a group of friends. If everybody else is telling stories about their dog, and you start talking about how good you are at basketball out of the blue, you haven't added to the conversation. In order to successfully participate, you should offer another dog story."[18]

"Yes, and ..." allows you to keep the flow going. However, when instead you say, "Yes, but ... ," that flow gets disrupted. Let's say you say to someone, "Boy, Joe Pardavila has a lot of great advice." And that person responds, "Yes, but he puts pineapple on pizza." Like our brain surgeon whose improv partner decided he wasn't a brain surgeon, you're left wondering what the heck to say next. However, if the response is instead, "Yes, and I like him even though he puts pineapple on pizza," you've reached for common ground and can continue to talk about how great I am. (Of course I don't really put pineapple on pizza. But even if I did, it's wrong to use pizza toppings as a dividing point.)

"Yes, and ..." is something I learned at UCB, but it actually predates that organization. It came out of Second City and other

---

17   Matt Besser, Ian Roberts, and Matt Walsh, *The Upright Citizens Brigade Comedy Improvisation Manual* (New York: Comedy Council of Nicea LLC, 2013), 9.

18   Ibid., p.12.

earlier improv groups. The power of this idea has lived on for decades, and it's an essential way of thinking that I take very seriously. So seriously that when one of the radio hosts I worked with routinely violated the idea, it started to put my nerves on edge.

You know how sometimes, in interviews, when someone is asked a question, the person says, "Hmmm … that's a good question." Well, here's the reality: Usually they don't really think it's a good question; they think it's a *tough* question. So they need a few seconds to think through how to answer it. Nothing wrong with that; give the person some space to say what they want to say.

But this particular host thought there *was* something wrong with that. He was too impatient. So when he asked someone something and the response was "That's a good question," he would immediately fire back, "Well, then *answer* it!"

For some reason he thought he was sooooo clever when he made that move. Me, I would grit my teeth and think to myself, "Don't you understand that the only reason that person is saying that is because they don't have an answer ready? And all you're doing is attacking them for that and making them defensive?"

By the way I'm not the only one who thinks "That's a good question" is a way to stall on answering. Former *Today Show* anchor Katie Couric in her book *Going There* has this to say about the late legal superstar attorney Johnny Cochran: "I'd interview Cochran multiple times, zeroing in on what he knew and when he knew it. He never tipped his hand. I could always tell he was stalling when he'd say, 'Katie, you know, that's a very good question.'"[19]

If a quick thinker like Johnny Cochran had to occasionally take a moment to gather his thoughts, what hope do the rest of us have? The fact is, not everybody is fast on the draw during an interview,

---

19   Katie Couric, *Going There* (Massachusetts: Little, Brown and Company, 2021), 219.

especially the ones we did, since many of those kinds of conversations happened so early in the morning. Even beyond the fact that they were expected to be sharp and funny at dawn, the truth is few people are going to be as quick-witted as talk show all-stars like Tom Hanks and Martin Short, people who can immediately throw out a hilarious, well-constructed answer to the most mundane question.

When you ask someone a question and they hem and haw a little, you need to give them a little time. If it's someone you know well and you can joke around their hesitation, it's no big deal, right? But when it's someone you don't know … well, shutting down the other person that way is just useless and counterproductive confrontation. It's not a "Yes, and …"; it's a "No f—ing way!"

You want to help a person through an interview or conversation, not stop them in their tracks. During the radio days, we would also talk to a lot of celebrities who were doing twenty interviews the same day to promote a project—naturally that left them a little frazzled. I always tried to consider factors like that because my thing is, you never know what's going on in the other person's life. They may be going through incredible stress and drama in their lives. They may just be having a really crappy day. Whatever the case, if they are struggling, the thing to do is make them as comfortable as possible and "Yes, and …" them to the finish line. If they're momentarily hesitant with a response, I like to say "Hey, you know what? Take your time answering that question." Or I'll explain the question a little bit more just to give the person a breath and gather their thoughts. There's no rush.

> *You want to help a person through an interview or conversation, not stop them in their tracks.*

Especially for me since I no longer have to break for commercials …

The Urgency of Urgency

Okay, so I just told you how to relax the other person in a conversation, how to "Yes, and …" them to put them at ease.

Now forget all that because we're about to talk about *urgency*.

My instructors at UCB did not include any household names from the world of comedy. The closest I came to having a famous teacher (besides Colin Jost's brother) was Anthony Atamanuik, who became renowned for his impression of Donald Trump. He even had his own series for a while, *The President Show*. But before all that, he was teaching UCB classes, and I vividly remember him saying to us right out of the gate, "I probably shouldn't be teaching a 101 class." He instantly looked like he regretted saying that, but he had been doing improv so long that he probably thought the 101 level was beneath him. He was probably right. The rest of my teachers didn't have his extensive experience—they had also come up through the UCB system I was currently learning.

But that extensive experience meant he had a lot of valuable insight to share. There was one piece of wisdom in particular I've never forgotten, and it became one of the best tools I use as an interviewer. What he told us is this: A scene you're going to perform from scratch with a partner has to be taking place *on the most important day of that person's life*. In other words you should give the scene that kind of incredibly heightened sense of urgency. It raises the stakes and causes the audience to sit up and take notice. The scene should be like one you'd see in a big-budget movie—something big is happening, and the audience is learning about it through your improv.

Now let's translate that idea into the art of conversation. If you're not putting that level of urgent energy into a back-and-forth, it's going to deteriorate into a meandering mess. Sometimes that's fine. I mean, if you're hanging out with friends or watching TV with your partner, nobody has to be working hard to deliver important-with-a-capital-I talk. But when, say, you're running a business meeting or making an important phone call, you want to communicate in a way that has impact. You have to show you care in a way that makes everyone else care. And if you can't convey that urgency, nobody else is going to be all that hyped about it. In short, it's about taking on an attitude that *what you're talking about matters*. A TV station once used the slogan, "We still treat news as if it matters." Well, theoretically, news should always matter, so maybe not the greatest tagline, but you can see what they were doing—they wanted to tap into that attitude of urgency I'm talking about.

Open Your Ears and Open Your Mind

Lastly, what UCB really did for me is to make me a better listener. Because you *have* to be. This is where how good you are at active listening really can make or break you.

The mark of a bad improviser is someone who, while their partner is talking, is thinking about something funny to say and, at the same time, completely missing what the other person is talking about in the scene. How can they respond in a logical way if they're not listening? Let's go back to the UCB Manual: "There is nothing more important than listening. The beginning of the scene is built with 'Yes, and …' and you cannot 'Yes, and …' something if you haven't heard it … if you don't actively listen at the beginning of a scene, you may think you're building a house out of straw, while your partner thinks you are building it with bricks."[20]

---

20   Matt Besser, Ian Roberts, and Matt Walsh, *The Upright Citizens Brigade Comedy Improvisation Manual.*

Again, this happens all the time in real life too. People have conversations with the aim of doing their own brain dump, not caring about what the other person has to say. Improv teaches you the exact opposite of that. You have to feed off the other person's remarks, and you can't do that unless you listen closely. That's the only way you can react honestly (and humorously) in the moment. When you want to control the conversation and have it only be what you want it to be, it's going to hinder any sort of bonding or spontaneity. "Yes, and ..." only works if you're listening and not thinking about what you want to say.

And by the way people get really pissed off when they feel like they're not being heard. How is that going to help you in a talk? It always reminds me of a scene in an old movie by the Coen Brothers (the guys who brought you *Fargo* and *The Big Lebowski*), *Barton Fink*. Barton Fink is a screenwriter who's self-obsessed, living in a rundown Hollywood hotel and never shutting up about himself to Charlie, the guy in the room next door, played by John Goodman. Near the end, Charlie turns out to be a homicidal maniac who burns down the hotel. C'mon, people, it happens. Anyway, as flames are roaring out of control in the hallway, when Charlie confronts Barton, Barton says meekly to him, "Why me?" And Goodman screams, "Because ... *you don't listen!*"

That's how angry not listening can make other people. I'm not saying they're gonna burn your house down, but ... well, keep a fire extinguisher handy if you frequently check out on someone.

UCB sadly had to shut down during the pandemic, but it's worthwhile remembering all the great talent that emerged from that improv giant over the years. We're talking Ilana Glazer and Abbi Jacobson from *Broad City*, Ellie Kemper from *Unbreakable Kimmy Schmidt*, Aubrey Plaza from *Parks and Recreation*, Donald Glover from *Community*, and many more. It's unfortunate UCB is gone from the scene now, but they gave me and a lot of other students and performers a great foundation for the future. I've only shared a few of their ideas in this chapter, but there's plenty more where that came from, so I suggest you check out their book, *The Upright Citizens Brigade Comedy Improvisation Manual*, if you want to know more.

Now it's time to leave the world of improv and get back to business. And to do that we have to turn the dial up to eleven. I'll tell you what that means in the next chapter.

CHAPTER 7

TAKE YOURSELF TO AN ELEVEN

HEIGHTEN YOUR PERSONALITY AND ELEVATE THE INTERVIEW

I'VE SEEN HOWARD STERN interviewed multiple times on different shows, and one thing he has said repeatedly always sticks with me. He says when he's doing his radio show, yes, it's still him … but at an exaggerated level.

And he's absolutely right. One of the tips I always give to people, whether they're podcasting or just facing an important conversation, is this: "Be yourself but at a spinal tap eleven." If you haven't seen the movie *This Is Spinal Tap* (and you should), it's a parody of a less-than-brilliant heavy metal group where the one guitarist wants the music so loud he gets an amp that goes up past the usual ten on the volume knob to an eleven. This scene assumed a life of its own outside of the movie, with "up to eleven" entering the *Oxford English Dictionary* in 2002.

Obviously when I say take yourself to an eleven, I'm not talking about the volume of your guitar. I'm talking in terms of a conversation. You want to become a higher level of yourself, enthusiastic and passionate, in order to gain the best results. You don't have to be a type A personality to pull this off—just think of it in terms of putting on your "happy face."

The best comparison I can make is how we talk to dogs or babies. We smile widely and pitch our voices to get their attention because, well, words aren't going to do the job since they don't know very many of them, if any. So we try to interact with them through upping our energy. Well, it's the same principle—if you keep your energy up, that energy will end up engaging the other person. (Just please don't use a falsetto voice to ask "Who's a good boy?" repeatedly—that doesn't work too well.)

Look, we're all human beings with a wide range of emotions. We sometimes feel down and irritable. I get it. But if you submit to that mood and bring that black cloud into an interview situation, it's going to affect the quality of the conversation. You've no doubt had people tell you, "Geez, I really blew that job interview. But I just felt so down walking into the room that I couldn't make it work." You probably have said something similar to yourself after a disappointing performance in, say, a meeting or talk.

So you have to fight off the gloom and lock onto the light. I will admit this can be hard to pull off. But talking for a living has taught me you *can* overcome a negative mood and make it work for you. On a personal level, it helps keep conversations positive and productive. On a professional level, it's a must and something even the biggest personalities on the planet must master.

Let me share a few examples.

As the Crowe Flies

Not sure if you are aware of this fact, but actor Russell Crowe is not known for his good nature. This is a man who has torn phones out of hotel walls and thrown them at the staff to make his extreme displeasure known.

So maybe, just maybe, all of us at 'PLJ were a wee bit nervous when Mr. Crowe came to town to be our in-studio guest. But then again we had already encountered our share of prickly celebrities, so how bad could it be? Besides, he was there to promote his rock band, 30 Odd Foot of Grunts (don't ask), so why wouldn't he want to come across as Mr. Congeniality?

Before his interview we invited him into a studio for what we call "liners" in the radio industry. I'm sure you've heard them before—they're short promotional bits where a popular entertainer gleefully states you're listening to their favorite radio station. (You'll often hear these play coming out of commercial breaks.) Russell agreed to do them. He sat down, and we handed him a paper with the liners we wanted him to read—again, it was just a couple of sentences. But instead of reading them, he searched the room then looked back at me. "Where are the headphones?" he asked.

Mind you, most celebs don't use headphones when they're guests because they usually don't want to mess up their hair. (Bruce Willis and Vin Diesel would be exceptions here.) So I didn't take him that seriously and jovially responded, "Oh, Mr. Crowe, you don't need headphones." His response? Not so jovial.

"If I didn't need fucking headphones, I wouldn't have asked for fucking headphones!"

Okay. So we now were officially worried about where this interview might end up. But we didn't have to be concerned. Crowe was a pro, so when he began talking with the whole team on the air, he was funny, honest, and open about his movie and fledgling music career. Good thing we got him those headphones.

This wasn't the last time I saw just how much negativity real stars were able to push past in order to show the public their best faces. Once, Jon Bon Jovi and Richie Sambora visited our studios to promote the latest album from their band Bon Jovi. These two had been recording music together for nearly thirty years, so you might think they were best buds. You would be wrong. Right before the interview, Richie and Jon had gone into separate rooms to handle some other media engagements. We were minutes from our on-air interview when we sent one of our assistants to fetch Jon. They respect-fully approached the rock and roll icon and said, "Mr. Bon Jovi, we're on air with you live in five minutes."

To which Jon replied, "Go get the guitarist," with a mock wave of his hand and an air of disdain that was definitely at an eleven.

"Go get the guitarist?" You mean the guy you've been making a lot of music and a lot of money with for the past three decades? Cold, dude.

But then, when it came to the actual interview, the two of them couldn't have acted chummier. They were finishing each other's sentences and cracking jokes, resulting in a fun, loose, and authentic chat. Before and after that chat was a completely different story, though. A few years later, Richie ended up leaving the band, giving as his official reason that he wanted to spend more time with his family. He only played with his old bandmate one other time, when Bon Jovi was inducted into the Rock and Roll Hall of Fame.

What can we learn from cranky celebrities? Just this: If they can overcome whatever crap they're going through and deliver a great interview, so can you. Leave your black cloud at the door and instead pretend something wonderful just happened, like you just won the lottery. Don't drag bad vibes into an interview because they'll bring it down one way or the other—either through you being low energy or ending up actually snapping at the other person. Put yourself in as good a frame of mind as possible before you do the talk.

Onward and Upward with Oprah

So yes, taking it to eleven is important in terms of your mood and energy. But that's not enough on its own. As a matter of fact, too much happy-happy can actually repel people. I think we've all seen enough loud, fast-talking people with frozen grins on their faces in the media to last a lifetime. So yes, you want to tackle the conversation with positivity, but no, you don't want to push it to the point where you transform yourself into a cartoon. You want to put yourself out there in an authentic way. In the stories about Russell Crowe and Jon Bon Jovi I just shared, you'll note I didn't mention they came across as fake or overly enthusiastic. What they did do was give us authentic and engaging talk. So when I say "take it to eleven," what I don't mean is you have to be louder or faster. It's really just more about presenting a heightened sense of who you are and ditching whatever negativity you're feeling at the moment. Todd Pettengill puts it like this:

> Anytime you walk in a studio anywhere, you become something of an actor. You're either selling a product or selling yourself. And who cares how you feel on that particular day, right? Nobody wants to hear you complain. The true key is to be relatable. Coaches tell you to be real. Well, you're already real, you don't have to try to be a real person.

In preparation for this book, I interviewed Sandy Girard, a podcast superstar. She's the head of programming for Crooked Media's current podcasts, which include *Pod Save America*, *Pod Save the World*, *Lovett or Leave It*, *What a Day*, *Pod Save the People*, *Keep It*, *Hysteria*, and more. We discussed people who come into the studio and focus way too much on their performance. Here's a snippet:

> Folks come in and they think they have to have a radio voice or think that they have to deliver a performance in a very specific way. I'm always like, no, people are going to want to know what you actually sound like, what you talk like, so don't adjust yourself. For the most part, people really want authenticity. For me, I'm always encouraging people to use their authentic voice.

You'll hear more from Sandy in a later chapter. For now, if you learn anything from this book (and God, I hope you do), it's this: In a conversation, *the other person has to be your primary focus, not you.* People who are too fixated on their own performance frequently have a difficult time connecting with others in interviews. It drives me crazy to see talk show hosts just asking random questions off the cards their producers prepared for them. That's not the job—creating *engagement* with the guests is. You should never ask questions for the sake of asking questions. Instead you should give them context and intent that taps into who the other person is.

In a conversation, the other person has to be your primary focus, not you.

The person who gave us all a master class in doing that is the one and only Oprah. Before she showed up on our TVs, talk shows offered pretty rudimentary interviews, mostly with celebrity guests discussing a project and dropping a few one-liners here and there. That began to change with Phil Donahue's talk show, the first one where the host actually walked through the audience with a mic and interacted with everyday people at a deeper level. Barbara Walters took it up another notch with her *20/20* interviews where she (gasp) would actually make other people cry with her probing questions.

But Oprah? She "just blew the whole thing open," according to Mary McNamara, a television critic at the *Los Angeles Times*.[21] "The only thing she was interested in was what made you feel, what made you cry, what you were scared of, what you were proud of. She was interviewing people as if she was talking to a child, getting to the bare emotional core."

You can't do what Oprah does without really locking in on who you're talking to. I mean, you still probably won't be able to do what Oprah does (who can?), but if you're 100 percent present and coming in at an eleven, you'll get as close as you can.

Mirror, Mirror

Let me throw one more big reason at you for bringing your best self to a conversation—a concept called *mirroring*. No, mirroring is not something the Kardashians do every other minute to check out their makeup. Mirroring is an ingrained human behavior in which one person unconsciously imitates the attitude, body language, and speech patterns of another. This may be more proof that we're descended from apes because mirroring is best summed up by the phrase "monkey see, monkey do." Our brains actually have these things called "mirror neurons," which enable us to observe other people's behavior, learn from it, and replicate it. It also helps us bond with other people because it teaches us empathy and helps us

---

21   Emily Sohn, "How Oprah Winfrey Changed America," NBC News, May 26, 2011, https://www.nbcnews.com/id/wbna43175402.

gain an understanding of others' emotions. And we continue to do it for the rest of our lives.

Now here's where this relates to the subject of this book—mirroring happens in almost every conversation. You smile, the other person smiles. You frown, the other person frowns. You scream an obscenity, the other person ... well, okay, mirroring only goes so far. But *this* is why you want to be at an eleven when you talk to someone. If you come in mopey with low energy, people are going to respond to you in a subdued way. They unconsciously mirror your mood, and the result probably won't work for either of you.

Your body language is also important in terms of mirroring. A study asked job interviewers to follow specific types of body language. One group of interviewers was told to demonstrate distant and uninterested body language (like avoiding eye contact or leaning away), and another group was asked to show more welcoming body language (smiling, making eye contact, etc.). In both cases the job applicant mirrored the interviewers' body language. And those who mirrored the less-friendly gestures and movements didn't do as well as those who mirrored the more welcoming movements.[22]

So mirroring matters, which is why the way you approach a conversation or interview matters. If I'm talking to a person who's crabby at the start, I don't let it throw me. Instead I stay enthusiastic, that enthusiasm becomes contagious, and eventually their mood brightens. It's one of my best interviewing hacks, and it almost always works.

And by the way, mirroring is a two-way street. When you mirror the person you're talking to, you can gain more of their trust and they'll be more open with you. This is a strategy that can easily be

---

22 Carl O. Word, Mark P. Zanna, and Joel Cooper, "The Nonverbal Mediation of Self-Fulfilling Prophecies in Interracial Interaction," *Journal of Experimental Social Psychology* 10, no. 2 (1974): 109–120, doi:10.1016/0022-1031(74)90059-6.

misused (a lot of lawyers do it and use the term "tactical empathy," which is a little creepy), but in general, some conscious mirroring can be done to help along the connection to the other person. It can be as simple as repeating their last phrase—they might say something like "So I had nowhere to go," and you respond with a sympathetic "You had nowhere to go" to indicate you're sympathizing with them, or you can just do something as simple as nodding along while they talk. Whatever the case, giving them affirmative body language will help make them feel secure in telling their stories and expressing what they feel. All you're doing through mirroring them is putting yourself on *their* level, so the bond strengthens.

Let's go back to Oprah. Part of the reason she is so effective is because of how she mirrors her interview subjects—it comes from a totally honest and genuine place. While talk show hosts like Maury Povich and Jerry Springer exploited people's intense emotions for the sake of ratings, Oprah took people's pain seriously and revealed her own in the process. A pivotal episode happened when she had guests who were victims of sexual abuse. During the frank conversation, Oprah shocked the world when she confessed that she too had been molested as a child. When she did that, she changed the nature of the talk show genre and put the topic of sexual abuse into the national conversation. With that admission she became one with her audience and her guests. She brought it all together by conquering her own shame and sharing something incredibly personal with the world, which, of course, helped other victims open up about their experiences and deal with them. She took it up to eleven in her own unique and unforgettable way.

And that's what I'd like you to take away from this chapter. Going to eleven doesn't mean shouting like you're a bad shock jock (which I never was) or an obnoxious pitchman on a commercial. It means being completely present and then some. Just be who you are, stay laser focused, and tune in to the emotions of whoever you're talking to. Who knows? Maybe you'll break new ground and get yourself up to a twelve.

Next up, I'm going to share the three most important words we used to abide by in the radio studio when it came to doing successful interviews. It's a process I still use for podcasts. So turn the page, keep reading, and soon you'll be able to deal with the likes of Russell Crowe and his fucking headphones.

CHAPTER 8

PREPARATION, CONCENTRATION, MODERATION

THE THREE MAGIC WORDS

LET'S START THIS CHAPTER with a hearty salute to Bill Drake.

I will now pause a moment for you to ask "Who?"

Bill Drake was a legendary Top 40 radio host who, back in the 1960s, changed the medium forever. He created a formula where on-air personalities made their talk more targeted (which also allowed them more time to play music). That formula lifted KHJ in Los Angeles from twelfth place to first, a feat duplicated by radio stations all across the country that were smart enough to sign on to Bill's new "Boss Radio" format.

No, you didn't pick up a history of Top 40 radio by mistake; there's a reason I'm telling you all this—because Bill Drake also created a very valuable mantra to keep radio hosts focused when they communicated in order to create a more streamlined and enjoyable experience for the listener. That mantra?

Preparation. Concentration. Moderation.

Bill called it "PCM," and it took on a life of its own. Scott Shannon, who was my mentor, saw Bill as his mentor and, in Bill's honor, made a sign that hung by the clock in our studio for years. Okay, it wasn't even really a sign; it was very DIY—the three PCM words were placed horizontally on a regular sheet of printer paper in a seventy-two-point font. But it was good enough to make us mindful of the PCM idea during every show we did.

To me, it's still the blueprint for successful communication, which is why I decided to devote a chapter to it. Before Bill drummed PCM into the brains of radio hosts coast-to-coast, they would blather on too long without a point. They were paid to talk, so … they talked. But most of it was too long and not all that good. Result? Listeners would spin the tune dial to find a station with hosts who *did* have a point.

Now I'm going to go out on a limb and assume you don't want anyone tuning you out when you talk, whether it's to an audience or your next-door neighbor. In this chapter we'll talk about how to help you avoid that fate by examining the ideas represented by PCM and why each word is important to your success in conversations and interviews. And as we talk about each of those words, I'll also share Scott's comments on what each of them means to him.

Preparation: Yes, You Still Have to Do Homework

To me, the most important letter in PCM is the first one. Preparation is vital to having the best possible conversation, something I found out early on.

When I was working my way up the ladder, one of the roles I had to take on was one part exhausting and one part gratifying—covering red-carpet events for media events. It was where I first learned the importance of preparing for interviews.

Ninety-nine percent of these events in person look nothing like what you see on television before a big entertainment event, like the Oscars or a premiere. They usually take place at a movie theater or a large venue, and they're overflowing with an army of journalists from all media, including TV, print, radio, and digital platforms. And these journalists aren't given the best treatment. At most of the events, it's the TV crews who get the best spots, the easiest access, and the most time with celebrities on the red carpet. For everyone else ... it's like *The Purge*. Everyone is jockeying for position at all costs.

And to make matters even more stressful, the most dangerous individuals on the red carpet are the paparazzi. Their general ethos is "Get the fuck out of my way," because they only get paid if they snap the right pictures.

Did I paint a wonderful picture of the glamorous world of red carpets?

Here's where it gets more fun. *Most of the reporters covering the red carpet don't know who anyone is*—unless it's someone who's huge. The most common question I would hear from the other media reporters was "Who's that?" It got so bad that the companies doing the events began putting together a sheet of mug shots of everyone who was invited to that event. That way, when the sixth lead from *One Tree Hill* showed up, the reporters knew who they were.

But I went beyond that because I found that the more research I did beforehand, the better chance I had of connecting with whatever media star wandered in front of me. It was a vital part of my success and a lesson I still haven't forgotten.

But some do.

Most of you know who Joe Rogan is. As I write this chapter, he's one of the most popular podcasters around as well as one of the most controversial. I'm not going to wade into some of the less-than-enlightened comments he's made over the years, but I will say this dude is genuinely great at having conversations with people from all walks of life—from cage fighters to scientists to movie stars. He knows how to do it, even if some of his ideas are a bit out there.

But, frankly, sometimes he misses the mark, as we all do from time to time. In 2021 Rogan had a fascinating and wide-ranging chat with CNN chief medical correspondent Dr. Sanjay Gupta about the COVID-19 pandemic. And while I was listening, I grew more and more irritated, not by anything Rogan said but about something he didn't say. Because during the first two hours of the three-hour conversation (yes, three hours), Gupta would occasionally interject with comments like "That's why I wrote this book" and "I talked about that in the book." Hint, hint, hint.

However, it took *two hours* until Rogan finally asked, "You have a new book?"

As I said, Gupta had already referenced the book multiple times before Rogan finally took note of it. If Rogan had done even minimal research before the show, he would *already have known* Gupta had just released a book. It would have taken a half-second on Google. Maybe three-quarters of a second on Bing. I am not standing by those numbers; I'm just saying you can find out things like that *really, really fast*.

Here's the bottom line. Even though you may no longer be in school, you still have to do your homework for interviews and important conversations. For instance, in a job interview, you better know something about the company going in, or you're going to look a little clueless. It comes down to showing *respect* for whoever you're interacting with. That doesn't mean just being nice and polite; it means taking the time to research them in advance so you go into the talk having a good understanding of what they're all about.

Marc Maron is another hugely popular podcaster who doesn't do much research on his guests and openly admits it. He says he just does "vague research—the type of research almost anyone could do."[23] But he believes not knowing too much keeps the conversation fresh. Generally, because he's so talented at talk, he makes it work for him, but frequently he won't know enough about a guest, and as a result he won't ask the kinds of questions he should. More importantly not taking the time to research a guest properly can offend that guest.

Case in point? When Maron interviewed the veteran watermelon-smashing comic Gallagher, who had recently come under fire for his act, which many thought was getting increasingly homophobic and racist. Maron, not knowing much about Gallagher except for all the recent negative buzz, became too confrontational too fast, causing Gallagher to throw a hissy fit and storm out of the recording session. The interview was never finished. Vulture.com, *New York* magazine's culture website, talked to Maron about this talk train wreck, which yielded this important observation: "Maron concedes that he did not handle Gallagher as well as he would have liked to, that he did not do a whole lot of research but instead was going off the current conception of Gallagher as a right-wing hate monger."[24]

The truth is Gallagher had enjoyed many years of popularity before he made this dark turn in his career. Maron not only didn't do

---

23 John Horn, "Marc Maron Talks about Resentment and How Everything Could Still Go Wrong," *The Frame*, May 13, 2015, https://archive.kpcc.org/programs/the-frame/2015/05/13/42816/marc-maron-talks-about-resentment-and-how-everythi/.

24 Nathan Rabin, "That Time Gallagher Displayed His True Awfulness and Then Stormed Out on Marc Maron," Vulture.com, November 16, 2015, https://www.vulture.com/2015/11/that-time-gallagher-displayed-his-true-awfulness-and-then-stormed-out-on-marc-maron.html.

the preparation, but, as we'll discuss in the next section of this chapter, he also didn't do the proper moderation within the interview. There are ways to talk about distasteful stuff and explore it intelligently without endorsing offensive viewpoints. An explosive conflict doesn't have to be inevitable. This is where Maron fell down on the job, and he knew it.

Everybody makes mistakes. I'm not saying Joe Rogan and Marc Maron are bad at their jobs. Hell, who can say that? Their continuing popularity indicates they're amazing communicators. What I am saying is they can get away with being lazy about their prep. Most others can't because they're not gifted enough to navigate in the dark like Rogan and Maron.

And let's be real about the research—you don't have to spend weeks or even days on it. If you're talking to an author, you don't have to read every single one of their books in advance. If they're an actor, you don't have to watch every single thing they've been in. Musician? Check out a few songs and you're good. Your goal should be to familiarize yourself with what they've done, sample some of it, and also take a look at their back story.

Again, it's about respect. Especially in a podcast situation, you should know who the guest is and, just as importantly, make time to talk about what *they* want to talk about. You've seen enough talk shows to know that Dwayne Johnson or Adele don't randomly go on *The Tonight Show* or *Good Morning America* if they don't have a project they want to promote. That's all they show up for. Recently I saw a Stephen Colbert episode where Paul Rudd was the guest. Somehow, during Rudd's second segment, Paul ended up giving Colbert a massage. It was funny, but then it seemed as though Rudd suddenly realized he hadn't mentioned the movie he was there to plug and was terrified he would run out of time. So during the massage,

Rudd began talking about his new film, which was a little weird but demonstrates that these people have an objective when they go on TV or any platform—they want the audience to know about their newest movie or show or podcast.

So be polite and ask your guest a question or two about their current "thing." Even if it's just a personal conversation, always ask the other person what's going on with them. If you insist on pursuing only your own agenda, you've got a good chance of alienating the other person. And you're cutting yourself off from having as full and memorable a conversation as possible.

Doing the right kind of prep always helps an interview. *Always.* For example, the more information you have, the more ways you can help move a conversation along. You should know enough about someone's background to the point where, the talk stalls, you can ask, "Okay, so you took these steps. Now so tell me what you did next." Then there are guests who get bogged down in the details of their own story. If you know they're getting close to a good part of their story, you can encourage them to jump ahead by saying something like "And then the weasel actually got in your pants, didn't it?"

Here's another trick you can have up your sleeve, especially if you're talking to someone who's in the public eye. This is a tactic I tell people when I coach them to interview someone on a podcast—go online and find a little factoid, a video, or a memorable quote from years ago.

> *The more information you have, the more ways you can help move a conversation along.*

It could have been from a decade ago, maybe even twenty years ago, but find whatever it is, make sure it isn't genuinely embarrassing, and bring it up with the person. The more obscure, the more impact it will have. And there will be an impact. That person will glow and say something like "Oh my god! You actually took the trouble to find that thing? I don't even remember that!" Not only does that help along a conversation, but it also makes the person 100 percent receptive to whatever you have to say because they're thinking to themselves, "Man, this son of a bitch did their homework. They didn't just show up cold to talk to me. They took time to get ready for this."

I always find that to be a great icebreaker. And you'll see the pros do it all the time. Some movie star will show up, and the host will play an old commercial they did when they were just starting out, and it just makes the conversation more enjoyable. It creates one of those "magic moments" we talked about in chapter 2.

And by the way you can also apply the same technique to a blind date or initial professional meeting. If you turn up something that's interesting but not embarrassing or horrible, bring it up and see what comes out of it. You're not only showing the person you cared enough to check them out, but you can also pivot to an interesting exchange you might not have had otherwise. We all google each other all the time these days, so it's not like you're stalking. Unless you're printing out all their social media posts and taping them to your bedroom wall. That *is* considered stalking, and I would stop that before the cops get involved.

One more thing on prep. A lot of people get intimidated when they have to interview an authority on something they literally know nothing about. I end up doing that a lot with the ForbesBooks podcasts I host. I'm talking to doctors, lawyers, scientists, CEOs, and I can't get away with just nodding, as that doesn't "read" well on a podcast. But you have to remember that person is the authority and you're not—they're (hopefully) going to take the ball and run with it. You just have to pass them that ball.

But you have to be at least familiar with their field.

What I do is learn enough about the subject matter in advance and use that info as a starting point to ask questions. From there, I just let the other person do the talking and continue leading them into areas that would be of interest to a general audience. And if they use jargon nobody outside their field would understand, I get them to explain what they're saying so everyone can get the meaning. In a way you're there to act as an interpreter, translating their specific fields of expertise to a wider audience.

Here's Scott Shannon on what preparation means to him:

> When you're looking at champions, you're looking at people who do plenty of preparation. Take Peyton Manning. When he went to Denver, one of the guys, one of the linemen, said, "I never met anybody like this in football before. He knew my job better than I knew. And I'm a lineman. He's a quarterback. He knew everybody's job on the team. And he read and he studied and he interviewed. He was friends with everybody so he could really lead the team." And that's exactly what Tom Brady did too. They say Tom Brady's the most prepared guy in football. And we all know how well he performed in so many Super Bowls.

Concentration: Stay Off Instagram. Also TikTok. Also Twitter.

Let's move on to our second magic word: concentration. Concentration means you put your entire mental energy into the conversation. You ask. You listen. You react. And you repeat. If Dr. Sanjay Gupta mentions his book, you act like you heard him. You also do your best to shut down distractions and interruptions in advance.

During the pandemic, YouTube amassed a huge collection of video clips featuring Zoom screwups that were broadcast live on national and international platforms. You no doubt watched a few of these as they were happening. I'm talking about experts whose cell phones ring or ding in the middle of talking (mute them before the call!), kids and pets who randomly barge in and disrupt (close the door or lock it if you can!), and of course that lawyer who famously couldn't figure out how to get rid of the cat filter over his face during a virtual legal proceeding.

I guess there's a case to be made that these unexpected problems were more entertaining than some of those conversations, but it's just not professional, especially if someone is a repeat offender. You must make concentration a priority, which is why your phone should be muted or, preferably, off and out of sight when you're in a conversation. Nothing ruins the flow more than a ringtone interruption (which just happened recently during a televised trial I was watching—and it was the judge's phone!). Disruptions can happen no matter what you do, but it's your job to at least try and minimize them.

But your real archenemy when it comes to concentration is your own brain. It's almost impossible for any of us to *not* be distracted these days. We're always checking out social media, email, texts on our phones as well as taking in media, news, and everything else we can do with those magical little boxes we hold in the palms of our hands. And the pace of everything is also a lot faster now. Watch an old movie or TV show and you'll almost fall asleep watching a character get out of a car, go up an elevator, and walk down a hallway before they get to where they were headed. Now the actor may pull up in front of the building ... and boom, the film cuts to him suddenly in an office confronting someone. A sequence that may have taken ten minutes in the old days now gets cut to the bone because producers know viewers are too impatient to watch all that.

Result? All of us now have the attention span of a fruit fly. That can't help but threaten our concentration. That's why before an interview or conversation, you have to temporarily clear your head of all the other million things that are bouncing around in your brain on a daily basis and only focus on what you're about to talk about. Think about it as emptying out all the trash in your computer's recycle bin.

My advice on how to build up your concentration skills? Go back to chapter 6 and read up on the improv training I recommended. Better yet, put it into practice. For example, I wrote about how you want to bring urgency to a conversation and pretend as though it's the most important talk you'll ever have in your life. It's self-applied pressure, and it works because it inspires the level of active listening you need to employ to really hear the other person and respond in an organic way.

Here's Scott Shannon on the importance of concentration:

When I golf, I used to think, "I have to make this putt, and then I'll have a birdie or a bogie or par. But if I miss it, my partner's going to be really mad at me, and we're going to be two holes down." But that's not what you do. You concentrate on the mechanics of making that putt. He said, when Michael Jordan went up for a shot or went up for a layup or a jump shot, Michael was different than the other people because he didn't worry about the clock. He didn't worry about what would happen if he missed the shot. He only focused on the mechanics of what he was doing.

Moderation: Don't Make Paris Cry

Imagine Paris Hilton, reality star and hotel heiress, in tears, crying and shaking … after a talk show appearance.

Who did this to her? None other than my talk show idol, David Letterman.

Paris went on his show in 2007, a few months after a brief stint in prison for driving with a suspended license. Letterman was the first interview she agreed to do after serving her time, with the stipulation that she wouldn't have to talk about her experience being behind bars. She was there to promote her new perfume (as I said people want to talk about what they want to talk about) and didn't want to dwell on that humiliating experience. As she said recently on her podcast, "My PR team made an agreement to him that it was off limits, and we would not discuss it, and we'd only be there to promote the perfume and my other business ventures. I felt like it was a safe place because I'd been going on *Letterman* for so many years, and he'd always have fun with me and joke around, and I thought he'd keep his word on this. And I was wrong."[25]

Letterman was relentless. Paris kept trying to duck and cover, but she couldn't stop him from returning again and again to her jail time.

"It was like he was purposely trying to humiliate me … After it ended, I looked at him and said, 'I'm never coming on this show again, you've crossed the line.'"[26] (By the way she was back on the show within six months, but then again a reality star needs on-air time like the rest of us need oxygen.)

What Letterman did was the opposite of what moderation should be. He pushed a guest on something she didn't want to talk about and continued to drill down on the subject. It made for good television, but it left a bad taste in a lot of people's mouths. Some hosts *do* push their guests' buttons on purpose, especially if it's someone they don't

---

25   Joey Nolfi, "Paris Hilton Reflects on Her 'Cruel and Very Mean' 2007 David Letterman Interview," *Entertainment Weekly*, March 2, 2021, https://ew.com/tv/paris-hilton-2007-david-letterman-interview-podcast/.

26   Ibid.

really like or have a huge disagreement with. Now sometimes a talk show is actually built around those kinds of personal clashes—if you ever watched Jerry Springer's or Maury Povich's shows, you get that. But you also get that those shows aren't exactly viewed as quality entertainment. They are to talk shows as pro wrestling is to sports—clown fests that may get good ratings but no respect. And you won't see any A-list celebrities popping up on them any time soon.

Which is why well-regarded hosts act fast to smooth over a distasteful incident. Even Letterman realized the error of his ways, no doubt because of the backlash from the public and the press. When Paris did return to the show, he handed her a giant bouquet of flowers and apologized profusely.

If you want to create or maintain a good relationship with whoever you're talking to, moderation is a must. What it comes down to is, you should host the conversation the same way you'd host a party. You want everyone to loosen up, have a good time, and trust that you'll treat them right. Like Paris, they want to feel like they're in a safe space and you're not going to do something crappy to them. If you want a metaphor, here it is—when your friend has a peanut allergy, you don't put out a bowl of mixed nuts.

You've probably heard the phrase "Everything in moderation." It's usually bad dieting advice. But when it comes to conversations, moderation is critical. You should explore sensitive subjects with discretion and pick up on when the

> *If you want to create or maintain a good relationship with whoever you're talking to, moderation is a must.*

other person is getting uncomfortable with a line of questioning. Put them at ease however possible. And give the talk room to breathe. No need to pepper them with rapid-fire questions—there's no shot clock in conversations or podcasts, for that matter. Instead keep the talk organic, make the guest feel respected and safe, and try out some of your meatier questions after they've loosened up. The more you push, the more they'll pull away.

And don't come down on a person just because you believe they're not delivering. Help them through the conversation as much as you can. And know that some people just aren't good at talking. Robert De Niro and Harrison Ford are famously bad interviews, throwing out monosyllabic answers that leave many a host scrambling to fill the time. But this is where preparation really can pay off. Because if you do enough research ahead of time, you'll figure out another topic to tap into, especially if you've written down enough questions in advance. As I said earlier in this book, I wouldn't be a prisoner to those questions—let the conversation unfold as naturally as possible. But if you need to tap into a new topic to keep things going, it's good to have them in your pocket.

Here's Scott's take on moderation:

Nobody wants to hear you drone on. We've all sat in audiences where somebody's talking or listened to a radio guy when he's talking away … and all of a sudden, your mind drifts to your family or your job or whatever.… Yeah, you're supposed to be listening, but it doesn't always work that way. Speeches can really be deadly. That's why when I do a speech, I try to shake the audience up. I'll say things like "I don't know why the hell I'm here today. I've never seen a bunch of bozos like you guys in one room, but I'm going to try to teach you something." I look for ways to get their attention and keep it.

So that's PCM. Following the sequence of preparation, concentration, and moderation will never steer you wrong—it's the perfect structure for a pro interview or a heavyweight conversation. By using PCM, I've been able to successfully talk to all kinds of people in all kinds of situations. But even I have my limits. My only caveat on guests? Never interview babies or CEOs. (I'm not talking about visionary founders, by the way, just suits who are all business.) They have nothing to say.

Up next, find out how Taylor Swift became my mortal enemy. I wish I could see you right now, furiously turning the page …

CHAPTER 9

AVOIDING DIALOGUE DISASTERS
SOME MORE "RULES OF THE ROAD"

I'M NOT PERFECT. I mean, you probably already guessed that by now. But did you know I was capable of pissing off one of the biggest celebrities on the planet?

I'm talking about Taylor Swift, who came into our studios for an interview once upon a time, which was a very big deal. Stay with me, this story is a little long, but it illustrates how making one stupid mistake before an interview even starts can screw up the whole thing.

At that time most of the biggest morning radio shows were being recorded on video and then posted online so fans could actually see their favorite stars be interviewed. The biggest of the big, Howard Stern, was one of the first to pioneer this practice. Naturally we wanted to video the Taylor Swift interview. But we were told by her team before she came in that we were only allowed to put the first five minutes of her interview on video.

This struck us as a little weird. We could video the whole interview but only post the first five minutes? Was she going to strip down to her underwear at minute six? Grow another head at minute seven? It seemed incredibly arbitrary to me at the time—as well as insanely irritating. But her team said, "Take it or leave it," and in my head I was thinking, "Fine," in that snarky way you use when you have to accept something you don't like.

Finally Taylor Swift came into the studio, and she was very sweet. Her publicist made a beeline for the videographer who shot the show for online. And just minutes before the interview was about to start, the publicist chirped, "Hey, guys, just a reminder, we're only going to shoot the first five minutes of this."

Oh.

So now we can't even video the rest of the interview? My irritation blossomed into annoyance and maybe just a hint of anger. In the back of my mind, I was thinking we'd be able to record the whole interview and maybe talk them into letting us use the whole thing. That option was suddenly off the table.

I tried a workaround. I asked, "Hey, just out of curiosity, near the end of that five minutes, if we ask a follow-up question to one of her answers, would it be okay to keep recording?" The publicist was a little flustered. She said, "Yeah, yeah. I mean, I guess so." And then I pushed a little harder. "And what if we have a follow-up question to that follow-up question, would we still be able to keep recording?" The publicist grew more confused. "Uh … yeah, I guess so."

And that was the point where Swift, listening to all this, figured out that I was being a dick.

"Well, somebody's being very saucy this morning," she said.

After that remark, I was smart enough to quit while I was ahead. However, the damage had been done. I was now on her radar and not in a good way. But then the interview started, and it went very well. There were about five of us in the room asking her questions. She was delightful, we were all laughing it up, everyone was having fun. But I couldn't help but notice that every time I was the one asking a question, she gave me a long, hard look as if she was waiting for me to say something horrible.

And I inadvertently ended up obliging her.

At the time of this interview, there was an Ebola scare in the city. Everyone's a little on edge about it. So I said to her, "You know, you're famously fan-friendly. You connect with them, you do public hugs with them. With Ebola out there, do you feel afraid to offer those hugs to people you don't know?"

She looked at me with pure hostility.

"No, why would I stop hugging my fans just because there's a very small chance of me getting something? No, full stop, I will not stop hugging my fans."

I dropped the subject. Mainly because I could see the daggers shooting out of her eyes. Did she think I was implying that all her followers were plague carriers? I don't know. I was lucky she didn't rally all the Swifties to come after me. Or write a ten-minute song about our break-up. But anyway there is a point to this story, and let's get to it.

Don't Ruin the Talk before the Talk

As the title of this chapter indicates, we're going to talk about how to avoid conversational train wrecks like the one you just read about. And the first thing we're going to address is how easily you can sabotage yourself in advance, like I did with Taylor Swift.

The great philosophers Iggy Azalea and Tinashe once sang "Dance like Nobody's Watching." And that's great. But I would also add, "Talk like everybody's listening." Look, I'm a huge fan of the

First Amendment, which gives us the right of free speech. It's up there with my love of the New York Mets, the New York Jets, and New York pizza. Unfortunately the First Amendment is the most misused one.

For context, the First Amendment reads like this: "Congress shall make no law respecting an establishment of religion or prohibiting the free exercise thereof; or abridging the freedom of speech, or of the press; or the right of the people peaceably to assemble, and to petition the Government for a redress of grievances." Short version? The government can't stop you from saying what you want to say, unless you're directly putting people in danger. (Yelling "Fire!" in a movie theater is the most referenced example of that.) Unfortunately some believe that it means "I can say whatever I want and not get fired, be made to feel embarrassed, or damage my reputation."

Yes, you have the right to say what you want. But other people also have the right to *react* to what you say however they want—they have free speech too. And that's the part most people forget. There are repercussions, and you have to deal with them. That's why when you're speaking anytime, anyplace … whether it's in a studio or out in public … whether it's being recorded (which these days is awfully hard to determine) … you want to be careful. You want to keep asking yourself, "What would I say if I knew *everybody* was listening?"

> Yes, you have the right to say what you want. But other people also have the right to react to what you say however they want—they have free speech too. And that's the part most people forget.

Or just Taylor Swift. I wasn't careful when I was going after the publicist to squeeze a few more minutes of video out of her. I didn't think about how the music superstar would react to that exchange. But of course she was listening to the whole thing—you don't get that kind of career without being very aware of what's going on around you—and it immediately made her feel defensive. So when I asked her what I thought was a fairly innocent question, she immediately thought I was up to no good.

Some of you reading this might think I'm advocating you censor yourself. Well, sometimes it's a good idea to do just that. This isn't about being "afraid" to be yourself. Go ahead and be yourself. If you like to take risks, go for it. But always know there could be consequences.

Let me tee up another celebrity story for you.

In the 1990s Michael Bolton became huge. He was known for his string of blockbuster hits, for dating Hollywood starlets, and ... for his fabulous hair. But over the years that fabulous hair went into retreat. Michael's hairline began to recede, and he was extremely sensitive about that fact.

But Todd, the radio host I produced the morning show for, didn't care about Michael's feelings. He started up a running gag on the air about how Bolton's hairline was starting to resemble that of the mostly bald comedian Gallagher, whom I mentioned in the last chapter. Now mind you, Todd was part of an NYC morning show that was listened to by millions of people in the tristate area, but for some reason he never assumed that a singer of the magnitude of Michael Bolton would ever hear about any of his cracks.

Fast-forward a few months and Michael Bolton generously agreed to participate in a promotional event for our listeners. Great! What could go wrong? Nothing, in our minds, because we had bought into Todd's assumption that Michael had never heard those Gallagher comparisons.

Well, the day of the event came around and Michael Bolton walked in. But he was not all that friendly. He asked to speak to the powers that be, and he informed them he would not be partaking in said promotional event. Unless …

Todd directly apologized to him.

Todd had no choice. Our listeners were patiently waiting to hear Michael Bolton. And again, Michael was very popular at the time. So Todd and Michael went into a room to settle their differences, and it wasn't pretty. Bolton went on a rambling rampage in which he asked Todd why he kept going after him. Did he ever steal Todd's girlfriend or knock a ball over Todd's head in a celebrity softball game? Why the hate? Why the hate?

How did Todd handle this blowback? Well, I'll let him tell you himself:

> I was told Bolton wanted me to apologize or he won't do the performance, and there are a hundred people in the next room waiting for him to show up. It'd be pretty selfish of me to say "F— off, Michael Bolton," and ruin their experience.
>
> So with the Michael Bolton thing, it was a very simple "Oh yeah, man. I'm sorry." And I knew him. I met him before he was anybody, and we played softball together, and that's why it was kind of strange. I thought he was doing a bit on me until we got in the room. But it wasn't. I mean, he was actually mad that I compared him to Gallagher. But you have to put the job first and eat a little crow. Just suck it up and take it.

Again, you never know who's listening. Todd sure didn't. Back then you didn't have to worry so much about getting caught saying something a little dicey because social media had yet to take over our lives. Now whenever anybody says something controversial, it instantly trends on Twitter, Facebook, or whatever social media platform you choose to participate in. And raising the stakes even more, sometimes the outrage is manufactured. We've all seen thirty-second audio and video clips get pulled out of context from much longer conversations and do instant damage to someone's reputation.

When you talk like everybody's listening, you safeguard yourself from most of that nonsense. When you don't ... well, saying something stupid and awful *will* come back to haunt you. Remember the heavily publicized search for a new host of *Jeopardy* after Alex Trebek passed away? The leading contender was the show's executive producer, Mike Richards—until some offensive remarks he made on a podcast years ago suddenly surfaced. Richards then deleted those online podcast files—talk about closing the barn door after all the horses get out— but it was no use. Not only did he not get the hosting job, but he also lost the producing job he already had. Something similar happened to a comedian named Shane Gillis. You haven't heard of him? Well, that's because he got fired from joining the *SNL* cast before he could even get on stage with them. Again, the culprit was a podcast in which he made racist and homophobic comments.

The list of people who have been "canceled" because of offensive remarks goes on and on. Again, they got to say what they wanted to say—the First Amendment was upheld. But the blowback caused their careers to crash and burn. Most legit companies don't want to be associated with those kinds of opinions, so they act quickly to burn those bridges.

As Scott Shannon once told me, you can't be a DJ without a microphone, so you want to make sure that microphone stays in your hands. You say the wrong thing and you can lose the mic in a split second. That's what happened to the people I've just discussed. They weren't victims; they were careless. They weren't talking as though everybody was listening.

The rest of us should.

The Science Is In

Most of the advice I'm sharing in this book comes from my years of experience conducting conversations. But there are actual people out there studying interactions from a scientific standpoint to figure out what can sabotage conversations. One of the top authorities in this subject at the moment is Dr. Alison Wood Brooks, who has a PhD as well as a sense of humor, as she often titles her talks "How to Talk Gooder." But make no mistake—this is an associate professor of business administration at the Harvard Business School, so she knows her stuff. With that in mind, I think it's important to share a few of her findings from her experiments in the rest of this chapter because they definitely ring true to me.

Let's run through two of the most important.

Topic Selection

Did you ever have trouble figuring out what to talk about with a person? Most of us have because, according to Dr. Brooks, most of us are horrible at it, especially when it comes to figuring out what the other person wants to talk about. (I'm talking to you, Joe Rogan—see last chapter.) Computers apparently are better at this than people—they can analyze the text of a conversation and figure this out with ease. Us? Our emotions get in the way.

You ever wonder why talking about the weather is so often a go-to? It's because people tend to talk about what's happening in their immediate environment. For example, if you're eating with someone in a restaurant, you inevitably end up talking about the food or the ambience or the decor. This is all well and good, except for the fact that you're not really engaging in any memorable conversation. The problem is we're all too damn polite. We can feel it's rude or abrupt to switch to another topic. So we hold back and keep talking about the humidity or something else just as lame. Not only that, we're also bad at brainstorming other things to talk about in the moment. So we move on from the humidity to what the chance of rain is tomorrow or whatever.

Well, Dr. Brooks analyzed two thousand business meetings (because she has the patience of a saint, I would reckon) and discovered the best meetings were ones that had a list of topics to be covered instead of being completely unstructured. She then discovered the same principle works in a normal conversation. If you go into one having two or three bullet-pointed topics in your head, the talk is much more engaging and productive.

As I've said, I go into interviews with this kind of tactic. I don't have a real set agenda; otherwise the conversation becomes overly structured and doesn't leave room for interesting tangents, but I'm always mindful of the areas I want to discuss in advance. Most people believe that thinking of topics in advance will result in an awkward or forced conversation, but that's just not the case. It just helps you keep the talk flowing.

Of course, in order to set topics for a conversation, you have to either know the other person or know something about them. But how do you handle it if, say, you sit down on a flight and feel like talking with the person who's in the seat next to you? Dr. Brooks took a group of people who were going to be in that situation and instructed half of them to switch topics frequently (whenever the conversation lagged). The other half? She gave no instructions at all. The first group ended up having more enjoyable interactions because of her directive. They were empowered to switch things up when the talk seemed to stagnate, and through that process they randomly hit on things the other person liked to talk about and tapped into them. The other group flailed like most people normally do when talking to a stranger.

To sum up, think of topics to talk about in advance when you're going to talk to people you know or know of. With people you don't know, be bold and spin the wheel of topics until you land on one that works for both of you. Again, this is science. But the good kind, where nothing will blow up in your face, unless you talk to Michael Bolton about his hairline.

Asking Questions

This is another subject near and dear to my heart. And the good doctor has identified the problem with how people deal with asking questions.

They don't do it.

Well, at least not as often as they should. There are two reasons for this. First, we're usually very focused on ourselves, so we frequently don't show the interest we should in the other person. The result is we neglect to ask them questions about themselves. Second, which we already encountered in Dr. Brooks's findings on selecting topics, we hold back from asking other people about themselves because we don't want to seem rude, intrusive, or downright nosy. (As I've mentioned, this is not a problem for *me*, but it is for most.)

In a conversation, instead of asking questions, most of us make *statements*. We're usually trying to persuade others into buying into our opinions or trying to show how smart we are. But sticking to flat-out declarations puts up roadblocks. The other person feels cut off because it feels like a conversation of one.

Dr. Brooks studied this issue through the lens of dating. Many a first date has resulted in one person angrily thinking to themselves, "He/She didn't ask me one question about myself!" So she looked at one thousand heterosexual speed dating interactions, recorded the conversations, had them transcribed, and studied how they went. What she discovered was simple and powerful—the more questions asked about the other person, the more likely a second date was. And this applied equally to men and women.

Then Dr. Brooks went big and analyzed five thousand sales calls. And she got the same outcome. The more questions a salesperson asked, the more likely the sale. The same went for entrepreneurs trying to entice investors into backing their businesses. It turned out that people even like online chatbots better when they ask more questions![27]

So asking questions is a great conversational secret to success. And here's another one—there's a *type* of question that works the best. Dr. Brooks calls it "magical." So abracadabra, here's what it is: *asking follow-up questions*. You ask a question, they answer, and you ask yet *another* question based on their answer. People love that because it shows you listened to what they said and responded accordingly. In other words, *you care*! And since we're all egotistical monsters, people care a lot about you caring! Follow-ups are quite simply the motor that keeps a conversation going.

> **Asking questions is a great conversational secret to success.**

For example, let's say Taylor Swift actually liked me (it's a huge leap) and responded to my Ebola question by saying, "Oh, I get what you're saying. But I have to hug my fans. I'm willing to take the chance." And then maybe I asked, "Why is this kind of connection to your fans so important to you?" And then we kept going from there—question, answer, question, answer, etc. Then maybe we got married. Okay, I'm getting carried away, but you see what I'm saying.

But let's change up this imaginary conversation. Let's say I didn't ask Taylor Swift a follow-up question. Let's say that I said after her

---

27 Rachel Layne, "Asking Questions Can Get You a Better Job or a Second Date," Harvard Business School, October 30, 2017, https://hbswk.hbs.edu/item/asking-questions-can-get-you-a-better-job-or-a-second-date.

response, "God, I'm not taking a chance. I read about Ebola. It's horrible." Well, I don't think she would really know what to say to that. I'm basically grabbing the spotlight, shining it on myself, and leaving her to shake her head sadly. Engagement off.

Brooks calls this kind of move a "boomer-ask." It's like a boomerang if it was made of words. You ask a question about the other person, the person answers, and you take that answer and bring it right back to yourself. In a normal conversation, that can stop the momentum of the talk as well as leave bruised feelings.

But the boomer-ask can sometimes be a good thing if you host a show or a podcast. Here's why. When you use the boomer-ask, you're getting some of your personality in the mix. And it helps you build up your authority to ask a question as well as build your online brand, which are important things for a host to do. Howard Stern, Joe Rogan, and Marc Maron are three examples of hosts who inject plenty of their own personality and experiences into their interviews. They *do* make it as much about themselves as the guest because their personalities are what keep people coming back for more—and that guest is not going to be back the next day. There's going to be another guest. The consistent thread is *the host*.

Successful hosts integrate their own stories with their own guests. For example, I might ask you a question about Mexico. As you go on about Mexico, I'm smiling inside. You see, I only asked that question because I have an *amazing* anecdote about that country in my back pocket that I'm going to pull out when the timing is right. But then I'm going to go right back to the guest and shine the light right back on them.

Face Time Is Better than FaceTime

Before we leave this chapter, there's one more thought I want to leave you with. And that's the fact that in this digital age, more and more we tend to have our conversations electronically, through texts, emails, and chats, rather than in person. I'm not going to play the grandpa who tells you that's wrong and how, in my day, you talked to a face, not a smart phone, dagnabbit. No, it's totally cool (and a lot more convenient) to communicate that way.

But there's one exception to that. If you're making a big ask or trying to persuade someone of something, you have a much better chance of making the sale if you do it in person, especially if you don't know the person that well or maybe not at all.

I once produced a podcast where the guest was Vanessa Bohns, a sociologist and professor at Cornell University (only the Ivy League for me). Bohns and her colleagues have done studies confirming the fact that people are less persuasive than they think they are over email.[28] How much less? Well, a request made in person was found to be *thirty-four times more successful* than one sent through email. It makes sense. People are more suspicious of an email request, so their empathy is diminished. This in turn holds them back from agreeing to what you want from them.

So when you want something from someone, show up in person to make the ask. They'll be able to judge your body language, your tone, and your facial expressions to judge if you're sincere or not. Whereas in an email, all they get is cold, hard words.

And if you're not sincere? Maybe stick to email.

In the next chapter, I'm going to talk strictly about podcasting. You'll learn more about the business behind podcasting and how to make sure yours is targeted for success.

---

28   Vanessa Bohns, "A Face-to-Face Request Is 34 Times More Successful than an Email," *Harvard Business Review*, April, 2017, https://www.researchgate.net/publication/320187671_A_Face-to-Face_Request_Is_34_Times_More_Successful_than_an_Email.

CHAPTER 10

THE YIN AND YANG OF PODCASTS
MASTERING THE NEW MEDIUM

HOW BIG ARE PODCASTS RIGHT NOW? Well, as of this writing, there are over *two million* different podcasts available for download from Apple (a quadruple increase from 2018), representing a library of over forty-eight million episodes.[29]

The audience is also growing by leaps and bounds. Back in 2015 only 17 percent of people had listened to a podcast within the past month. Now? That number has mushroomed to 41 percent, according to Pew Research.[30]

And then there's the bottom line, the real determinant of this new medium's success. Financially, podcasts are also becoming much more lucrative. The Interactive Advertising Bureau predicts that podcast ad

---

29   Ross Winn, "2021 Podcast Stats & Facts," *Podcast Insights*, August 25, 2021, https://www.podcastinsights.com/podcast-statistics/.

30   "Audio and Podcasting Fact Sheet," Pew Research Center, June 29, 2021, https://www.pewresearch.org/journalism/fact-sheet/audio-and-podcasting/.

revenue in the United States will hit $2 billion by 2023.[31]

So far this book has been full of advice that can apply to any conversation. But with podcasts on the upswing, this last chapter is designed to help anyone either contemplating making a podcast or who's already in the game. I've learned a lot in my new career as podcast director for ForbesBooks, and I'll be sharing more tips and tricks in this chapter. And if I'm not enough for you, then worry not—you'll also be hearing from some brilliant, high-level podcast executives I've had the privilege of interviewing.

The Big Transition

Terrestrial radio (AM/FM) used to be the dominant cultural force when it came to listening to something while you drove, went for a run, or maybe just relaxed in your backyard. Obviously that has changed. Satellite radio is now a major player as well as podcasts ever since Howard Stern jumped ship.

Still, 83 percent of Americans say they've listened to a terrestrial radio station in the past week.[32] In other words there's still a substantial pool of radio listeners. The problem is that pool is aging—most listeners are over fifty years old.[33] That fact alone explains the rapid decline of radio more than anything else. If you know anything about advertisers, you know they're hungry for the twenty-five to fifty-four age group. The result? Radio can no longer attract as much revenue as

---

31 Peter White, "Podcast Ad Revenue to Hit $2B by 2023, Says IAB," Deadline.com, May 12, 2021, https://deadline.com/2021/05/podcast-revenue-to-hit-2b-by-2023-iab-1234754426/.

32 "Audio and Podcasting Fact Sheet," Pew Research Center, June 29, 2021, https://www.pewresearch.org/journalism/fact-sheet/audio-and-podcasting/.

33 "Weekly Radio Reach in the United States in the 1st quarter of 2019, by Age Group," Statista, June 8, 2021, https://www.statista.com/statistics/468371/radio-reach-usa/.

podcasts. Which is why the former powerhouse NYC station I used to work for is now just a satellite station that plays prerecorded Christian programming—there's not much New York attached to what WPLJ actually does any more.

What really helped spike podcast popularity was the pandemic—people were stuck in their homes and apartments with little to do for months on end. And many discovered the allure of podcasts, simply because they needed to fill up their days with *something*. So podcasts not only bumped up their total listenership, but they also secured a pivotal place in popular culture. For instance, Steve Martin, Martin Short, and Selena Gomez hit a major homerun with their 2021 streaming series, *Only Murders in the Building*, built around the three stars doing—what else?—their own podcast.

My old boss Todd saw it all happen and has this to say about why podcasting has overtaken radio:

> Content delivery has changed, but content is still king. And especially now, where radio is still just reactive as opposed to proactive. Podcasters are taking content and delivering it in a different way and giving up on this whole idea that music and content go together—because they just don't anymore. You don't need to listen to six songs you don't like to get to one that you do. Or to get to the weather or the traffic or that interview the hosts have been hyping for an hour. You just don't.

So, yes, podcasting is having a moment. Not only are more people listening, but more are also producing them—because frankly they're not that hard to make. The technical side isn't that pricey or that complicated. But here's a hard truth: Don't imagine you're going to sit down, record your own podcast, put it out there for download, and then millions of dollars will start flowing into your bank account. As you might have already gleaned, there's a ton of competition out there. That makes it difficult (but not impossible) to compete with the heavy hitters, especially if you're not putting out a professional and targeted product.

There are two huge considerations you have to deal with if you want to do a podcast—the creative side and the business side, what I call the yin and yang of podcasts. In my mind the "yin" is making a quality product that delivers a great listening experience. We'll tackle that part first. And then we'll shift to the "yang" of it all, which to me is the business side, something you can't brush off as irrelevant if you're looking to make bank. This is where you'll hear about the realities of podcasting for profit from those podcast executives I mentioned earlier.

So let's jump in.

Be Peloton, Not Planet Fitness!

I've been using the word "audience" to describe the listeners of a podcast. That's how we measure the numbers. But when you're producing a podcast, you should try to forget that word and go beyond those numbers. The word you should be using is "community."

Audience vs. community. What's the difference? Well, there's a big one. An audience passively consumes entertainment and information. A community actively *engages* with it. The analogy I like to make is to the fitness world because … why not?

You've heard of Peloton, no doubt, if just from their relentless marketing. You've seen the commercials—they sell exercise bikes with screens where instructors can yell at you as you ride through the Andes Mountains or wherever. You've probably *also* heard of Planet Fitness, the chain of gyms and fitness centers that are currently in over two thousand locations in the United States.

So here's the question: Which would you rather be—Peloton or Planet Fitness?

I realize probably absolutely nobody has asked you this before, but there is a right answer and a wrong answer. Before you respond, let me throw a couple more stats your way. Peloton has 2.33 million connected members.[34] Planet Fitness has 14 million members.[35]

"Wow," you're probably saying to yourself, "I want to be Planet Fitness!"

Sorry, dude, that's the wrong answer.

Here's the thing: Peloton members are thoroughly invested in the brand. They buy the gear, constantly talk to their friends about it, and encourage others to try. They even share their progress on social media (no matter what Peloton's stock price is or which TV character is killed off while riding a Peloton as you read this). Whereas people who join Planet Fitness show up after the holidays and forget they're members by Valentine's Day.

See the difference? When you truly engage your audience and find ways to connect with them, as Peloton does, you build a community, *your* community, composed of people who will go out of their way to listen to your podcast whenever a new episode drops. An audience, in contrast, might listen to one podcast and never think of downloading another episode. They never felt the passion required that would drive them back to it.

---

34   Brian Dean, "Peloton Subscriber and Revenue Statistics (2021)," Backlinko, January 6, 2022, https://backlinko.com/peloton-users.

35   "Planet Fitness, Inc. Announces Third Quarter 2020 Results," Planet Fitness, November 5, 2020, https://investor.planetfitness.com/investors/press-releases/ press-release-details/2020/Planet-Fitness-Inc.-Announces-Third-Quarter-2020-Re- sults/default.aspx#:~:text=As%20of%20September%2030,%202020,%20Planet%20 Fitness%20had%20more%20than,,%20Panama,%20Mexico%20and%20Australia.

Here's another way of framing it from Dan Meisner, the director of audience development for Pacific Content, a leading podcast services company. Dan says you shouldn't ask how to build *an* audience for your new podcast. You should be asking how to build *your* audience. It's the same philosophy as audience vs. community. You want to attract faithful fans who want to enthusiastically engage with your content rather than what I call tourists—the kind of lookie-loos who will maybe check out your podcast once or twice and then move on.

> **When you truly engage your audience and find ways to connect with them, you build a community, your community, composed of people who will go out of their way to listen to your podcast whenever a new episode drops.**

That means, from the get-go, you have to define who your community will be composed of and how you can attract them. Start by asking yourself these questions:

- Who are we trying to serve?

- What do we know about them?

- What problems do they have?

- What are they clamoring for?

- How do we already engage them?

- How are they underserved by the current podcast market?

- What can we offer that they can't get anywhere else?[36]

If your show isn't designed for a *specific target audience*, you'll find it hard to get any traction. If it is, however, you have the opportunity

---

36   Dan Misener, "How Do I Build an Audience for My Podcast?" Pacific Content, January 30, 2020, https://blog.pacific-content.com/how-do-i-build-an-audience-for-my-podcast-c78f1152957c.

to create loyal and passionate followers who will come back week after week—in other words, that community I talked about.

It's best if you focus on subject matter you're genuinely interested in because your enthusiasm will come through and energize the show. It will also set it apart from any competition that might have similar content but lack the passion that's necessary to keep people engaged. For example, they may latch onto a currently hot topic that they think will get them listeners, but they're personally not that invested in it. People can smell that type of apathy from a mile away. But if you truly care about what you're doing, it's likely the listeners will too.

However, passion by itself isn't enough. You also have to be professional.

I mentioned Marc Maron a couple of chapters ago. What I didn't note then was that he was a *huge* pioneer in the podcasting world. When he started his podcast *WTF* in 2009, he was desperate, a washed-up stand-up comic hitting middle age with no plan B. Then he noticed a blip on his show biz radar—podcasts were just beginning to pop. Luckily he was finishing up a radio gig when he decided to try doing one, so he sneaked into his employer's studio after hours to do the first few episodes. When his radio contract was up, he fixed up his garage, set up the necessary equipment, and started interviewing people there.

Again, podcasts were barely anything back then, but he put everything into his show, and you could feel it. He talked openly about his troubled life and battles with addiction and had candid and intimate conversations with guests in which they revealed sides of themselves you never knew they had. The result was listeners became completely engaged with this offbeat guy that most of them had probably never heard of. His guest lineup was initially composed of his lower-tier comedian friends, but these days he has the likes of Barack Obama and Bruce Springsteen coming in for a chat, reflecting his hard-won status as one of the leading and most influential podcasters in the country. How influential? He and his producer would be the recipients of the first-ever Governors Award by the Podcast Academy for Excellence in Audio for their work on *WTF*.[37]

Maron's passion was on display from episode one, but so was his professionalism. He had a big advantage entering this brave new world because he was an expert communicator, a talent honed by years of doing stand-up. He knew when to talk, when to shut up, when to keep something going, and when to switch it up because he intuitively understood when people would probably get bored. In other words he didn't need this book.

But you probably do.

To build a better podcast, you want to up your communication skills by putting to work all the stuff we've been talking about on the way to this last chapter. But fortunately the podcast provides you with a very important advantage that you don't have when you're doing a speech or an interview live …

You can *edit*.

"We'll Fix It in Post"

I've shared a lot of screwups that happened during my years doing live radio. Those are going to happen no matter how good a radio host you are because you're broadcasting in real time, and unless you're Tony Stark, you really can't rewind the clock and fix bad things that already happened. (See *Avengers: Endgame* if you don't understand what I'm

---

37   Marianne Garvey, "'WTF with Marc Maron' Awarded the Governors Award by the Podcast Academy," CNN, April 12, 2021, https://edition.cnn.com/2021/04/12/entertainment/marc-maron-wtf-podcast-award/index.html.

talking about. Tony solves all the mysteries of time and space in about two seconds.)

Anyway, goofs happened on a regular basis during our morning show at 'PLJ because very little of the show was prerecorded. Sometimes a celebrity couldn't do an interview during the show, and we had to do it in advance. When that happened, we would edit the interview (if we had the time) and get rid of slow spots, mistakes, and anything else we thought would help keep the interview flowing smoothly. Because ... we could.

And with your podcast, you can too. So learn how to use this special power from the get-go. If I was starting out and didn't have a lot of experience, I might produce a handful of podcast episodes before I released even one of them. Instead I would go back and listen to them to make sure they worked. If they didn't, I wouldn't be afraid to start from scratch and do them over. But if they *sort of* worked, I'd rerecord some parts and boot up my editing program to make them as good as they could be.

"We'll fix it in post" is a common refrain when you're producing anything, whether it's a TV show, a movie, or a podcast. It refers to the fact that you have the time and the ability to fix any problems in postproduction (i.e., editing). Do-overs are a wonderful thing. Trust me on this. As I write this book, I'm rewriting over and over to make it the best it can be.

The fact that you can edit a podcast also helps you in another important way—you have the time to relax your guest before an interview, especially those who (a) have never done a podcast before and (b) are terrified they'll embarrass themselves. When I'm the producer, I stress to them that the podcast is being recorded in advance so they shouldn't feel like they're Nik Wallenda tiptoeing across a tightrope strung between two skyscrapers without a harness.

In the case of the podcast, there is a net to catch them if they fall, and it's a big one.

Don't get me wrong—you shouldn't lean too hard on your ability to edit after the fact. In other words don't skip doing the necessary prep work and also know that if the interview doesn't go smoothly, all the editing in the world might not make it sound right. If it requires a lot of surgery, it could end up sounding disjointed or unnatural. But little fixes here and there usually won't be obvious. And just knowing some level of redo is possible can make your guest (and you, for that matter) feel more relaxed about the experience.

That's why I say to newbies, "Don't think about anything else during the interview. Don't think about how bad you think you sound or how things might not be coming across. After we record the interview, we can get together and do a pick-up session where you'll get the chance to redo anything you want." As it happens, most guests don't ask for big changes. After they listen, most say, "I'm fine with the interview." But psychologically they feel looser and more comfortable knowing they can have a second chance if something goes wrong.

However, I've also had the opposite happen. I've had people who wanted to redo basically 75 percent of their interview because they didn't think they did as well as they could. Most of the time, *I'm* the one thinking that the interview was fine, but I also want to make sure they're happy with the end product.

Avoid the Big Ask

Sometimes I have to coach people who are going to *host* a podcast for the first time. In those cases I focus on teaching them how to ask questions, which, yes, we dealt with earlier in this book, but with podcasting you have to up your game a little more. For example, I specifically tell first-time hosts to avoid long questions. To me, if you ask, say, a six-sentence question, you're painting yourself in a corner. It leaves you no room to ad-lib, change things up, or do a callback to a previous point. It just doesn't work. And frequently the person you're talking to can't even keep track of what question you're asking. Have you ever heard a talk show guest say, after the host makes a long, rambling query, "Is there a question in there?" It's their way of saying, "What the hell are you talking about?"

Long questions contain too much information and too many words—they end up baffling the guest. And there's no reason for it. A question on a podcast should be no more than two sentences. That gives you room to play around with it and is easily understood by the interviewee.

Another no-no? Two-part questions. *Never* ask two-part questions on a podcast. Watch talk shows, news shows, interview shows, or even a press conference, and you'll notice how often two-part questions crash and burn. The person on the other side will usually just answer one part, especially if they don't want to answer the other part. And after they do that, both of you might forget what the other part of the question was.

You want to simplify questions as much as possible. The only two-part questions should end with something like "If yes, why?" In other words you should only use a second question that's meant to pull more words out of the person regarding the first question. Otherwise you're yanking the person in two directions at once. Think about the response you tend to get when you've sent a long email to someone who's extremely busy. They'll usually tap out three or four words as an answer to one or two points and fail to respond to the bulk of what you wanted to find out. They don't have time to read a novel in email form.

One more word of personal advice. A lot of beginning podcasters see what the big YouTube stars are doing (and naturally the money they're making) and believe if they video the podcast as well as record the audio, they can hit a home run with their very first swing.

My opinion? If you're podcasting for the first time, *wait* to add a video component.

To keep going with the baseball analogy, it's like you want to start out in the major leagues without going through the minors. You need to have some experience under your belt before you start worrying about video. By trying to focus on how you look at the same time you're trying to focus on how you sound ... well, that takes time. For example, when you first start out, you'll no doubt be looking down a lot of the time, referring to your notes. That ain't very camera-friendly.

With video, you also have to worry about your "look"—wearing the right thing, applying makeup the right way (if you use it), making sure your hair doesn't look like you were just in a tornado, stuff like that. Attending to all that takes some of your focus away from conducting a memorable conversation. It's too much of a distraction, at least until you feel comfortable interviewing to the point where it's almost second nature. Maybe down the line, the video component will work for you, but wait until you really know what you're doing with the podcast itself. If the interview is with someone who's remote, go ahead and make it a video call if you think it will help you two connect better, but just use it for that purpose.

One more big tip: Let your guests do the heavy lifting. Do your prep, but when the interview starts, tee them up with open-ended questions that will motivate them to talk at length on their specialty. You just need to know enough to ask the right things. They have to be the expert, not you.

Everything in chapter 8 ("Preparation, Concentration, Moderation") should be a big help to you in conducting your interviews. Balance professionalism with personality, and find ways to motivate your guests in advance so you can get the most out of them. In other words, stay out of the weeds, keep your energy up, and find memorable, punchy, and succinct ways to convey your information. It's good for them and good for you as host.

The Business of Podcasting

So we just talked about the yin of podcasting—the creative side. Now let's tackle the yang, the business side. Since this part is not my specialty, I'm going to share the wisdom of a couple of high-level experts in the podcast world. These are people who think about podcasts from a business POV. That's their job, and it's an important side of the process to understand. I've edited these comments for clarity because ... well, I can!

First up, Sandy Girard, executive vice president at Crooked Media, who first popped up back in chapter 7. Here's how she sees the dynamic of the podcast boom:

Balance professionalism with personality and find ways to motivate your guests in advance so you can get the most out of them.

> What's really sort of changed the game and put audio on the map in a different way in the form of podcasts is probably just the proliferation of devices and internet accessibility. We're all so dependent on our phones, and I think having on-demand audio in the form of podcasts has really helped proliferate that use because of the convenience and compatibility nature of audio, right? It's different than watching videos, where

you actually have to have even more reliable and faster speed internet and have more time to really be paying attention. As you know, audio is a lean-back medium. It's the companion that's always taking you to work every day or home, picking up your kids from school, or wherever you're driving.

But the truth is, especially now, it's harder than ever to create a hit. It's harder than ever to break through the noise. But I do think the entry point is a lot easier for most people. I think what people have realized is when you're in, it's like, oh, what is the purpose of me doing this? Am I going to be able to monetize this? Am I actually going to reach audiences? Or maybe you're not looking for a mass scale. Maybe you're looking to really target. If you are able to hit the audience that you're trying to reach, maybe you're creating something that's superniche and doesn't exist anywhere else. I think the beauty of the podcast space has been you can explore all these unchartered places and have conversations that could be very targeted. You're not trying to hit fifty million people because this is a conversation that's going to hit a subset of a subset of a subset.

Me again. What Sandy is getting at is the idea of connecting to a community that's interested in your subject matter. But it takes time to make that happen. My feeling is you can't realistically expect your podcast to pop after six months or even a year. If it does, congrats. Just know it could be a couple of years before you even know you have what's considered a hit in podcast circles.

And that's when you'll be ready to contact my next podcast expert, Dan Granger, CEO of Oxford Road. Dan operates in a space we haven't really discussed yet—podcasting advertising. He's been helping monetize podcasts since 2012, so he's an expert on what works and what doesn't in terms of attracting advertiser dollars. Dan, like me, is a radio veteran and can speak to the evolution of podcasting from that standpoint. And again he's a big proponent of creating a community of listeners rather than an audience.

Here's Dan's take on how podcasts have changed the media landscape:

> When you worked in local radio, you only had a limited range of topics that you could really go into and be commercially viable. What was fascinating about the fragmentation of media, and podcasting being a part of that fragmentation, was that you could now really narrowcast and build a tribe, a community, by talking about something that was really, really specific.
>
> One of my first clients ever in local radio was LegalZoom. I started working with them in like 2004 when they were just a scrappy start-up, scared out of their minds to spend $2,000 a week on an ad program. And guess what we did? Put them on a local radio show that was nationally syndicated, but it was a legal radio show. But you couldn't scale that, you couldn't find a way to target enough programming that was talking about subject matter that related to the product, it never would've been commercially viable. Podcasts opened that up, so that now all of a sudden, you could have a hundred shows with legal content and really tie it in a way that you couldn't before. So we can now narrowcast to people's interests, and that's great for advertisers, and it's certainly great for consumers. We all love it.

Who do advertisers want to reach with podcasts? I'm glad you asked ... because Dan knows.

Advertisers want high-value listeners. But I think it depends too much on income and education. If the consumer is too young to be viable for most of the products and services that we help to advertise, usually they're old enough to have a credit card or else they'd be on TikTok or YouTube ... but the reality is advertisers want the twenty-five to fifty-four demographic. Yes, you're starting to see people in their sixties get more active, but people who listen to podcasts are a little more advanced technologically, a little bit more innovative, a little bit more open to new ideas.

As you probably know, podcast hosts read most of the commercials themselves. And advertisers love it when those hosts are truly *influencers*. So ... try and become one. If you create a podcast that establishes you as a likable, attractive personality and/or a credible and reputable authority in your subject matter, then advertisers would love to have you read their ads, especially if their products are related to your podcast content. It's also fun for the audience when you have a little fun by ad-libbing a little during the commercial (Conan O'Brien is a master at this) as long as you're respectful of the product or service.

Here's Dan again:

You know, something else to remember about podcasts that make them super unique as a media channel is they're all comprised of influencers. That's all the real estate. So you don't buy an ad that gets inserted as much. At least that's not common practice yet. It will be more so, but right now, when you buy an ad, it's almost assumed that the personality who hosts the program is going to be doing the ad for you. And that's unique in a long form and attractive to an advertiser.

The business side of podcasts is much like the business side of *anything*. You have to create a quality product and build a following to succeed. That takes time and commitment. If you want to be a podcast pro, you have to have passion, drive, and maybe above all else, patience. It's not going to happen overnight. But when it does happen, you'll be the talk of the town—hey, maybe even the world.

SIMPLE AWARENESS

IN 2005 THE LATE GREAT WRITER David Foster Wallace gave a commencement speech at Kenyon College that has been widely heralded as one of the best ever given.

He began it this way:

> There are these two young fish swimming along and they happen to meet an older fish swimming the other way, who nods at them and says "Morning, boys. How's the water?" And the two young fish swim on for a bit, and then eventually one of them looks over at the other and goes "What the hell is water?"

DFW went on to explain the point of the fish story—that the "*most obvious, important realities are often the ones that are hardest to see and talk about.*" He went on to say people get obsessed with stuff beyond their own reality. For example, they want the answer to the biggest question of all—is there life after death? DFW thought that focus is a little misguided.

The capital-T Truth is about life before death.

It is about the real value of a real education, which has almost nothing to do with knowledge, and everything to do with simple awareness; awareness of what is so real and essential, so hidden in plain sight all around us, all the time, that we have to keep reminding ourselves over and over:

"This is water."

"This is water."

What does this story have to do with successful communication? Two words in that excerpt from the speech—"simple awareness."

Have you ever been sitting on a relatively deserted beach and suddenly a family of fourteen sidles up a foot away from your blanket and umbrella, even though they could have easily just sat in a spot ten feet away? Or in a very empty movie theater where a guy with a giant tub of popcorn and vat of soda sits two seats away, so you get to hear him munch and guzzle through the whole film?

Then you understand when someone lacks simple awareness.

If there's one huge takeaway I'd like you to gain from reading this book, it's that simple awareness is essential to successful conversations, whether it's a podcast interview, a work discussion, or just a random conversation with your partner. Being aware of who the other person is and the signals they're putting out, what you want to talk about, what they want to talk about, and the environment in which you're communicating ... these are all things that matter a great deal and can make or break a talk. And if you have an audience, you have to be aware of the signals they're sending out as well.

So be aware, read the room, and know that this is the water you're swimming in.

Years ago I read the book *The Secret*. It was a huge deal at the time. And it gave me a very valuable piece of advice I've used over the years. It's nothing about the law of attraction, which *The Secret* was based on, where if you think of something you want, you'll magically get it. No, it's something much simpler and easy to do. And it's this: Send people away on a positive note. Brighten their spirits just a bit.

That's why when I finish a conversation, I simply say, "God bless you. Have a great day." I'm not super religious or anything, but if someone seems like they're having a bad day and I say that to them? They smile and thank me. It's almost like me leaving a tip at a restaurant, only it literally costs me nothing.

Simple awareness is essential to successful conversations, whether it's a podcast interview, a work discussion, or just a random conversation with your partner.

The goal of a conversation should be a win-win, where everyone involved gains something from it. By maintaining simple awareness, it can happen.

I hope you've enjoyed reading this book and learned from it. Here's to you creating your own "good listen." If you want to connect, feel free to follow me at @joepardavila on Twitter, LinkedIn, and Instagram.

ACKNOWLEDGMENTS

OVER THE COURSE of my twenty years of working in the number-one media market in the world, I only shed a tear once while doing a show. It was during my final moments on 95.5 'PLJ. It wasn't because I was soon to be unemployed, it was because all at once I remembered all the people who helped shape me into the person I am today on and off the air.

I want to thank those friends, family members, and collaborators.

I must start with my wife, Theresa (or she would be really mad at me), because her companionship, love, and advice has been an integral part of my life. It continues to be an awesome ride with no end in sight!

Scott Shannon and Todd Pettengill, I am grateful for the opportunity you gave me and the mentoring you provided.

The amazing broadcasters I've had the privilege to have worked with daily: Jayde Donovan, Joe Nolan, Patty Steele, Bill Evans, Cooper Lawrence, and Anne Marie Leamy.

Suits sometimes get a bad rap, but I'm proud to have worked with broadcast executives like Tom Cuddy, Mitch Dolan, Stu Weiss, Tony Mascaro, and Gillette.

My radio brotherhood: Race Taylor, Louie Diaz, Dan Kelly, John "Kato" Machay, and Al Bandiero.

Arturo, who is a great big brother and an even better father.

And lastly my mother Maria. She never cared about what her sons did for a living, only that we were good people. I hope we lived up to her expectations.

DONE-FOR-YOU PODCASTING SERVICES

IF YOU'VE HAD LAUNCHING your own podcast on your to-do list but don't know how to get started, let Advantage Audio or Forbes-Books Audio help. We help you create twelve fifteen- to thirty-minute podcast episodes, which will be published twice a month. You select the topic and guests of the podcast; we coordinate logistics, book the guest, edit, and publish the show to all audio platforms. Our web team creates a landing page for your podcast so listeners and guests can find all episodes and learn more about your podcast and guests. Plus you'll have access to a podcast advisor for tips and help with the production aspects of the podcast. You'll be a podcasting pro in no time.

**VISIT ADVANTAGEFAMILY.COM/PRODUCTS/PODCASTING
TO FIND OUT MORE.**

9 781642 253849